The Boy, the mole, the fox and the Horse.

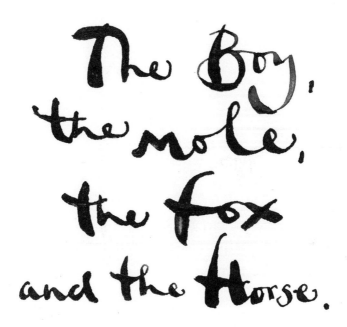

This book is dedicated
to my lovely kind mum,
and my wonderful dog
Dill.

THE BOY, THE MOLE, THE FOX AND THE HORSE

Charlie Mackesy

HarperOne

An Imprint of HarperCollinsPublishers

Hello

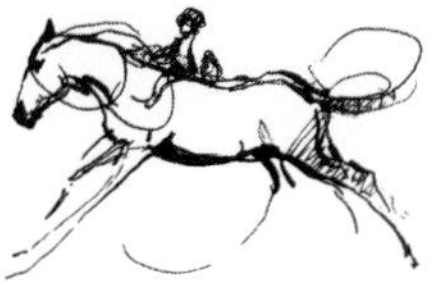

You started at the Beginning, which is impressive. I usually start in the middle, and never read introductions. It's surprising that I've made a book because I'm not good at reading them. The truth is I need pictures, they are like islands, places to get to in a sea of words.

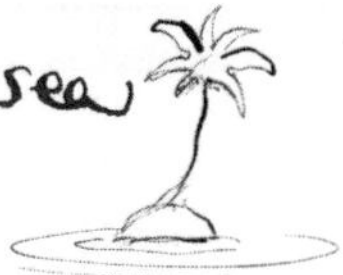

This book is for everyone, whether you are eighty or eight – I feel like I'm both sometimes. I'd like it to be one you can dip into anywhere, anytime. Start in the middle, if you like. Scribble on it, crease the corners and leave it well thumbed.

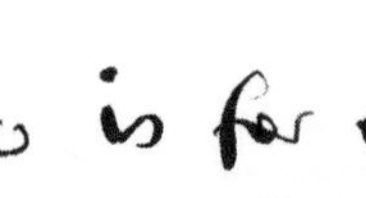

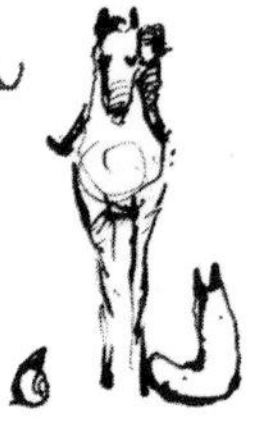

The drawings are mainly of a boy, a mole, a fox and a horse. I'll tell you a little bit about them – although I'm sure you'll see things here that I don't, so I'll be quick.

The boy is lonely when the mole first surfaces. They spend time together gazing into the wild. I think the wild is a bit like life – frightening sometimes but beautiful.

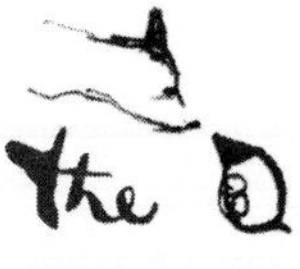

In their wanderings they meet the fox. It's never going to be easy meeting a fox if you're a mole.

The boy is full of questions, the mole is greedy for cake. The fox is mainly silent and wary because he's been hurt by life.

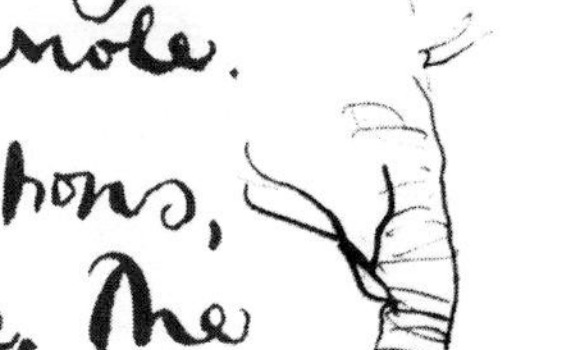

The horse is the biggest thing they have ever encountered, and also the gentlest.

They are all different, like us, and each has their own weaknesses. I can see myself in all four of them, perhaps you can too.

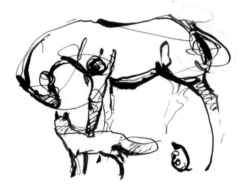

Their adventures happen in Springtime where one moment snow is falling and the sun shines the next, which is also a little bit like life - it can turn on a sixpence.

I hope this book encourages you, perhaps, to live courageously with more kindness for yourself and for others. And to ask for help when you need it - which is always a brave thing to do.

When I was making the book I often wondered, who on earth am I to be doing this? But as the horse says:

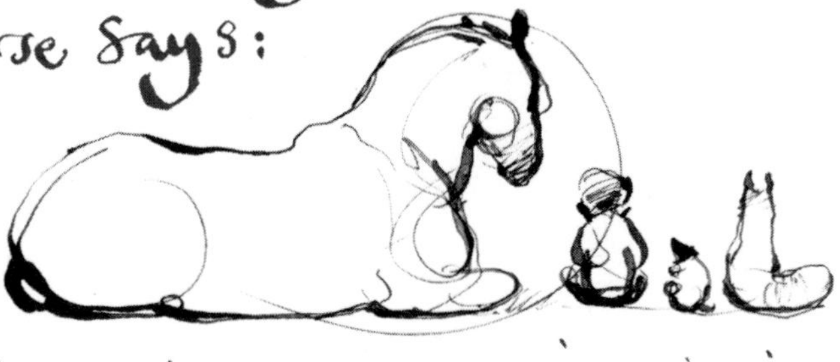

"the truth is everyone is winging it."

So I say spread your wings and follow your dreams - this book is one of mine. I hope you enjoy it and much love to you.

Thankyou. Charlie x

"Hello"

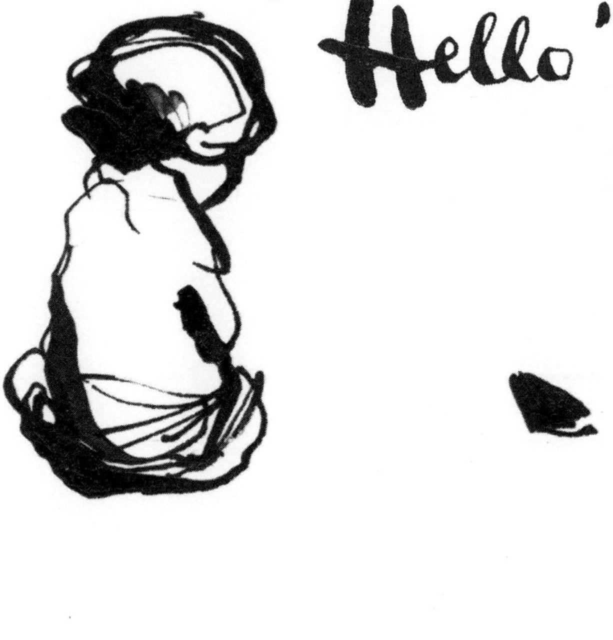

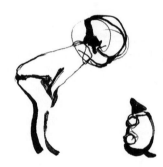

"I'm so small," said
the mole.

"Yes," said
the boy.
" but you
make a huge
difference."

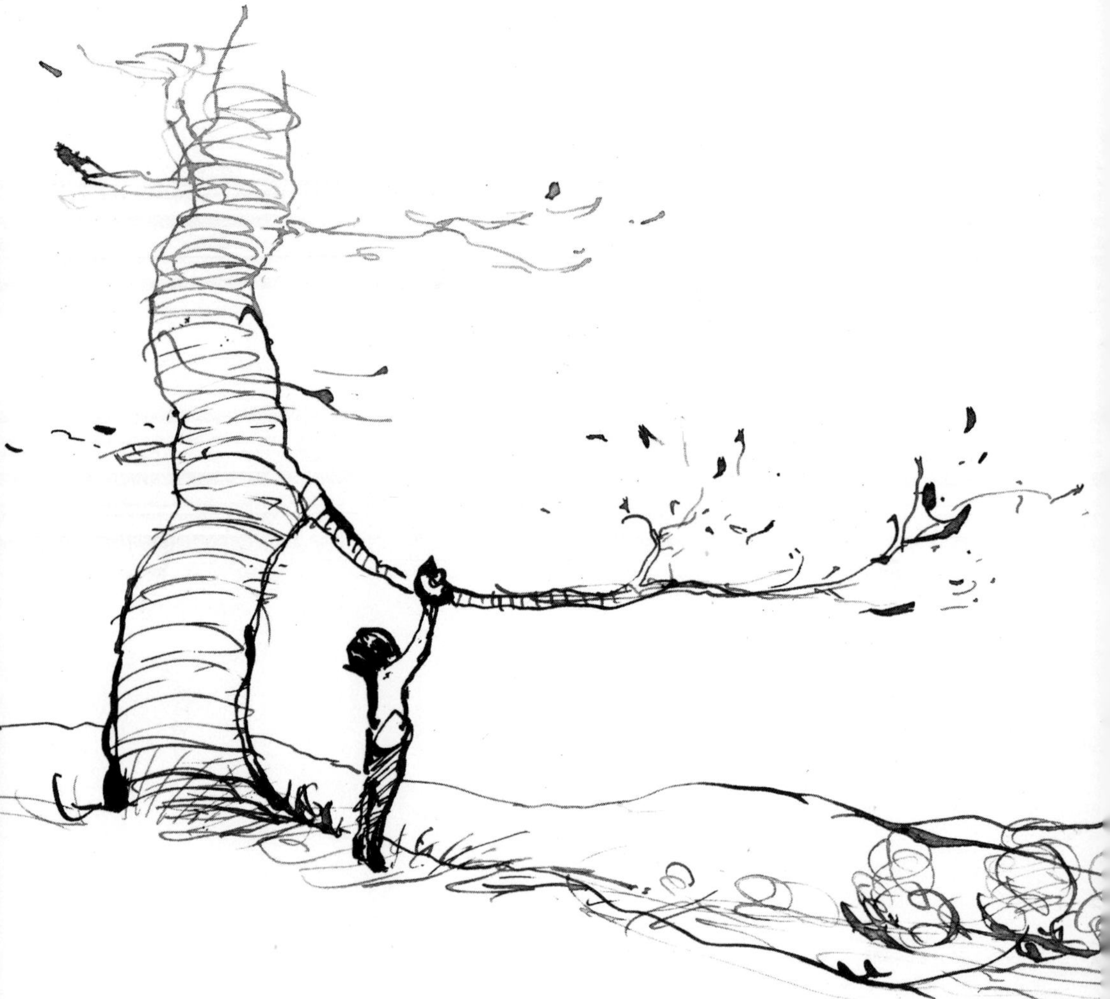

"What do you want to be when you grow up?"

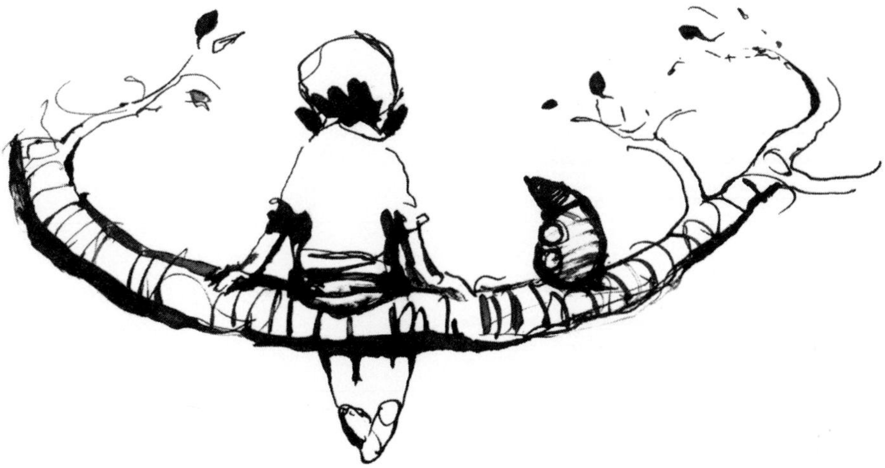

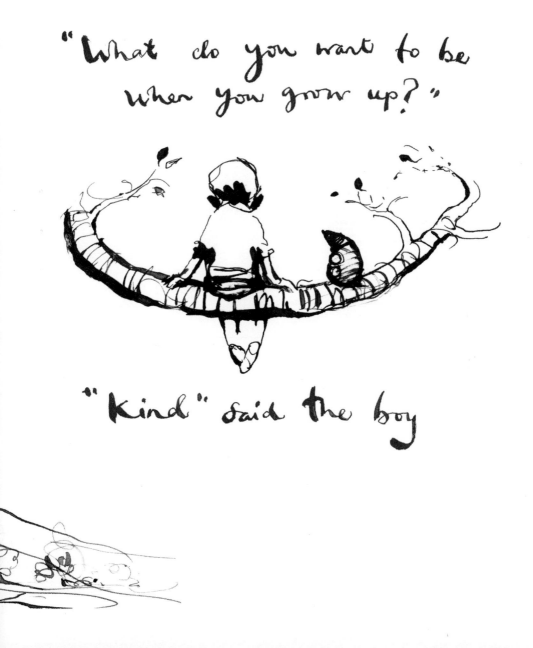

"Kind" said the boy

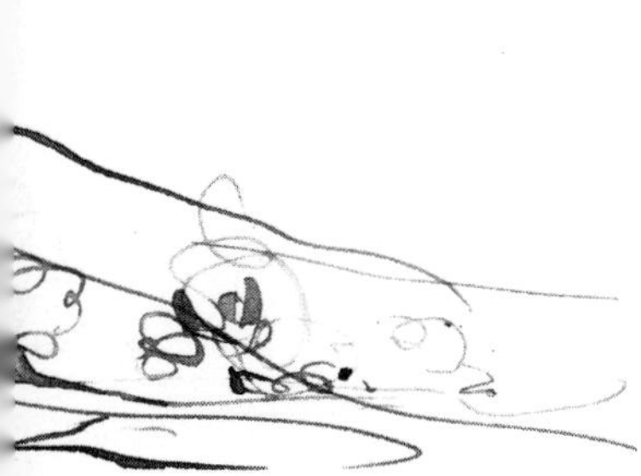

"What do you think success is?" asked the boy

"To love," said the Mole

"Well hello"

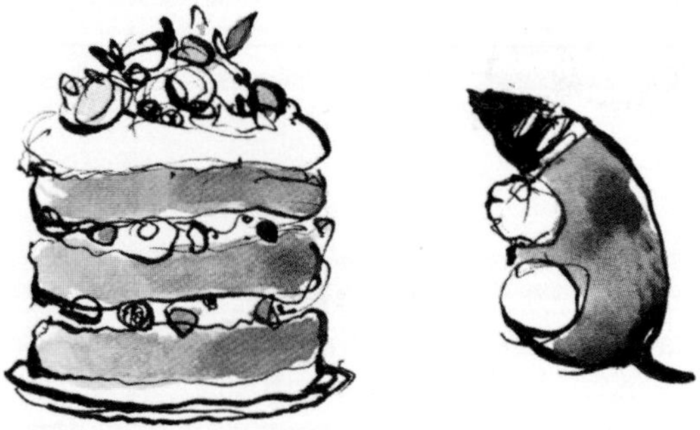

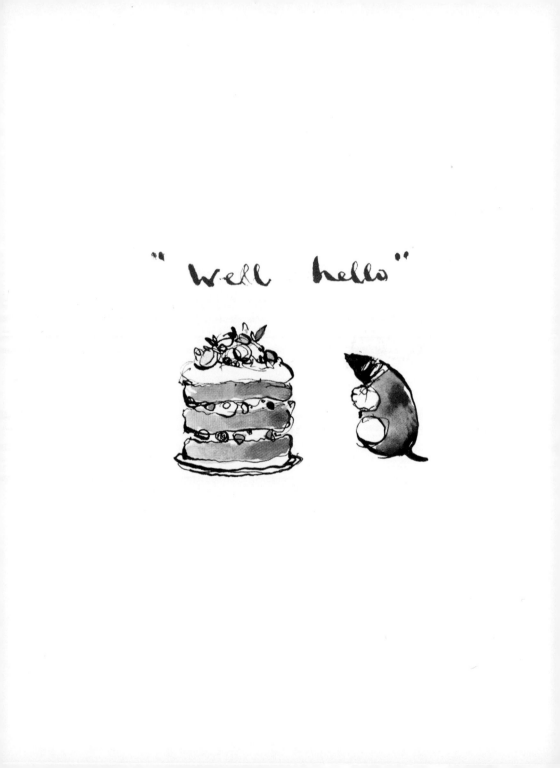

"Do you have a favourite saying?" asked the boy.

"Yes" said the mole

"What is it?"

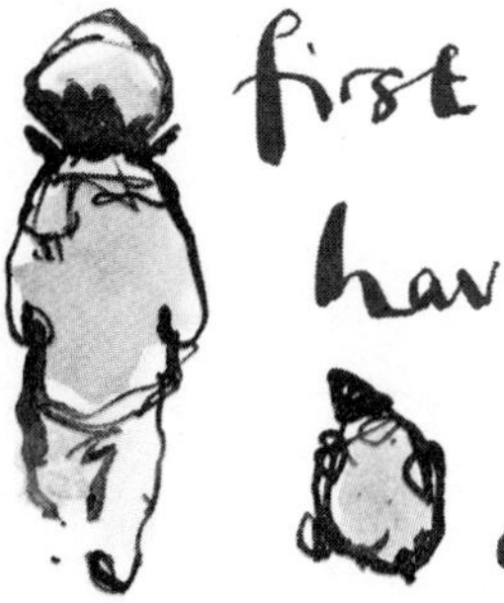

"If at first you don't succeed, have some cake."

"I see, does it work?"

"Every time."

"Just a tiny taste"

"I got you a delicious
cake," said the mole.
"Did you?"
"Yes"
"Where is it?"
"I ate it," said the mole.
"Oh."

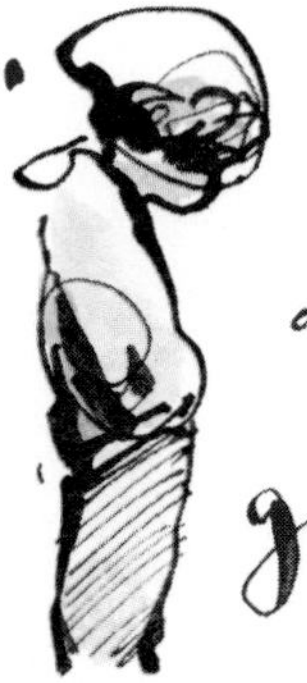

"But I got you another."

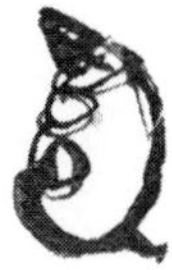

"Did you?
Where is that one?"
"The same thing seems to
have happened."

"What do you think is the biggest waste of time?"

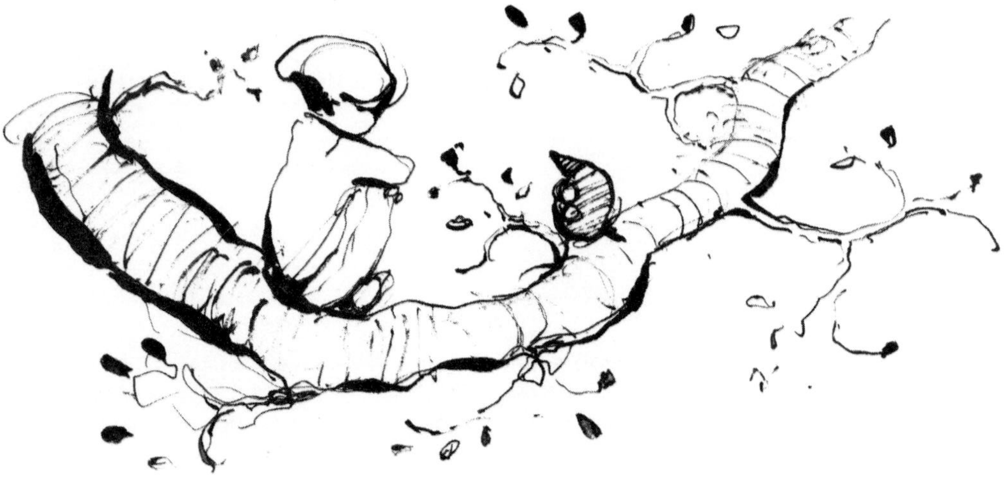

"Comparing yourself to others," said the mole.

"I wonder if there is a school of unlearning"

"Most of the old moles
I know wish they had
listened less to their fears and
more to their dreams."

"What is that over there?"

"It's the wild," said the mole
"Don't fear it."

" Imagine how we would be
if we were less afraid."

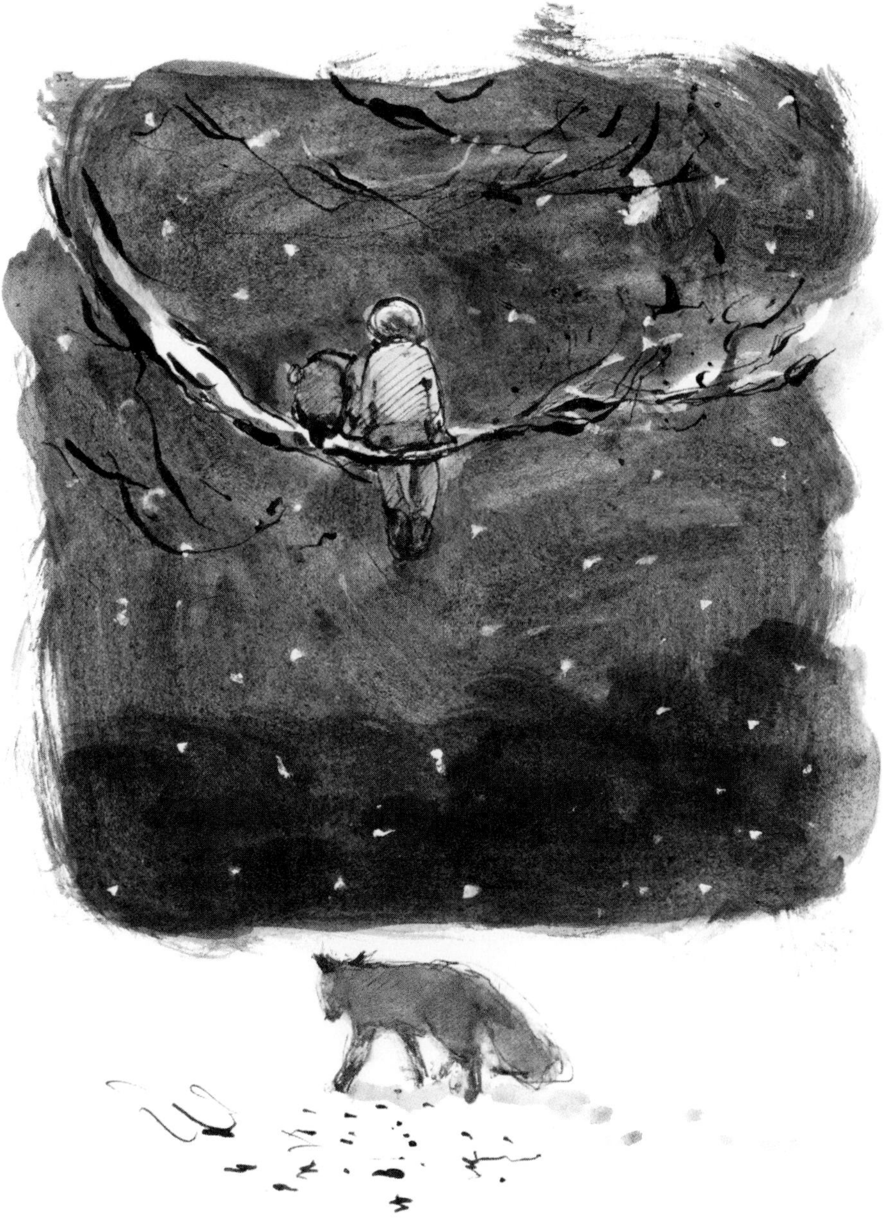

"I'm not afraid," said the mole.

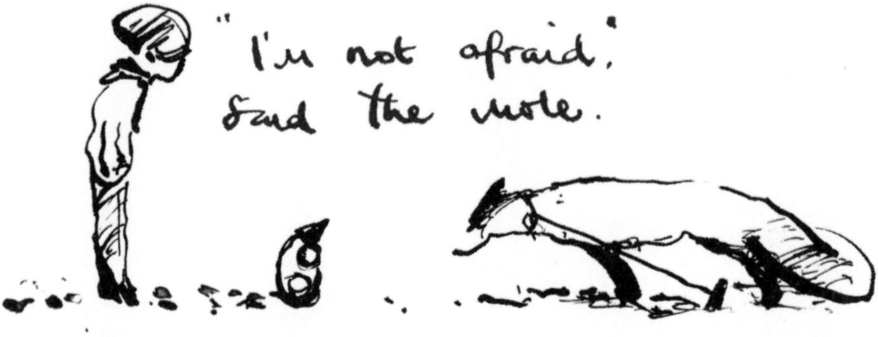

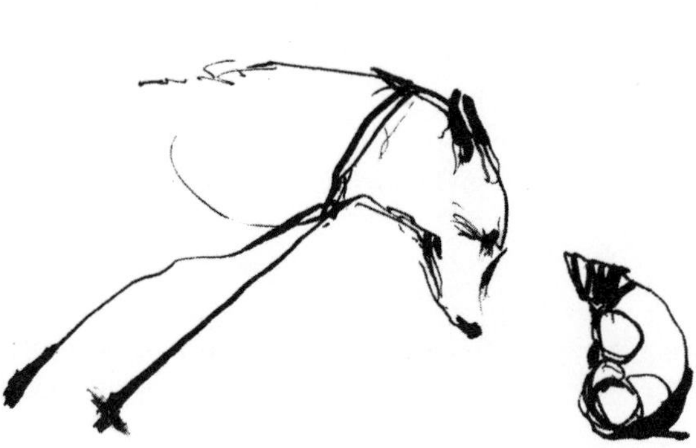

"If I wasn't caught in this snare I'd kill you," said the fox.

"If you stay in that snare you will die," said the mole.

So the mole chewed through the wire with his tiny teeth.

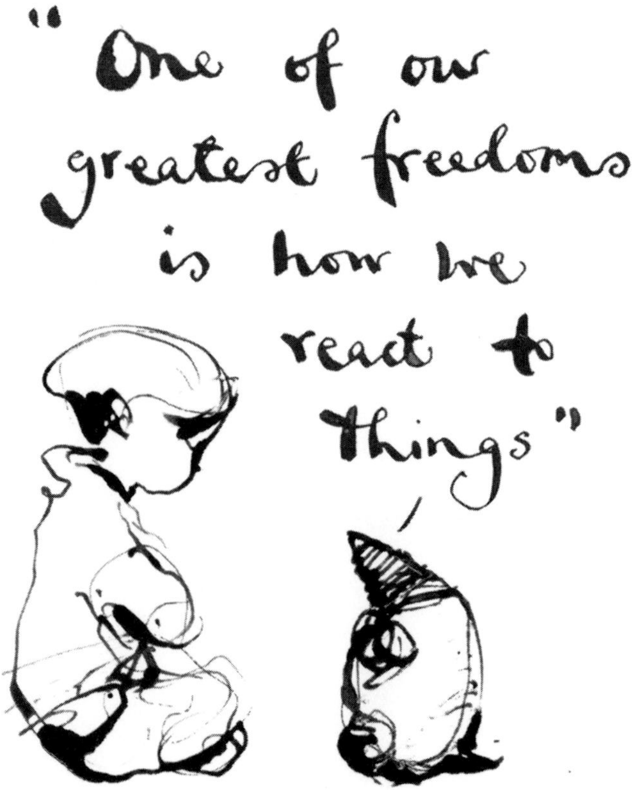
"One of our
greatest freedoms
is how we
react to
things"

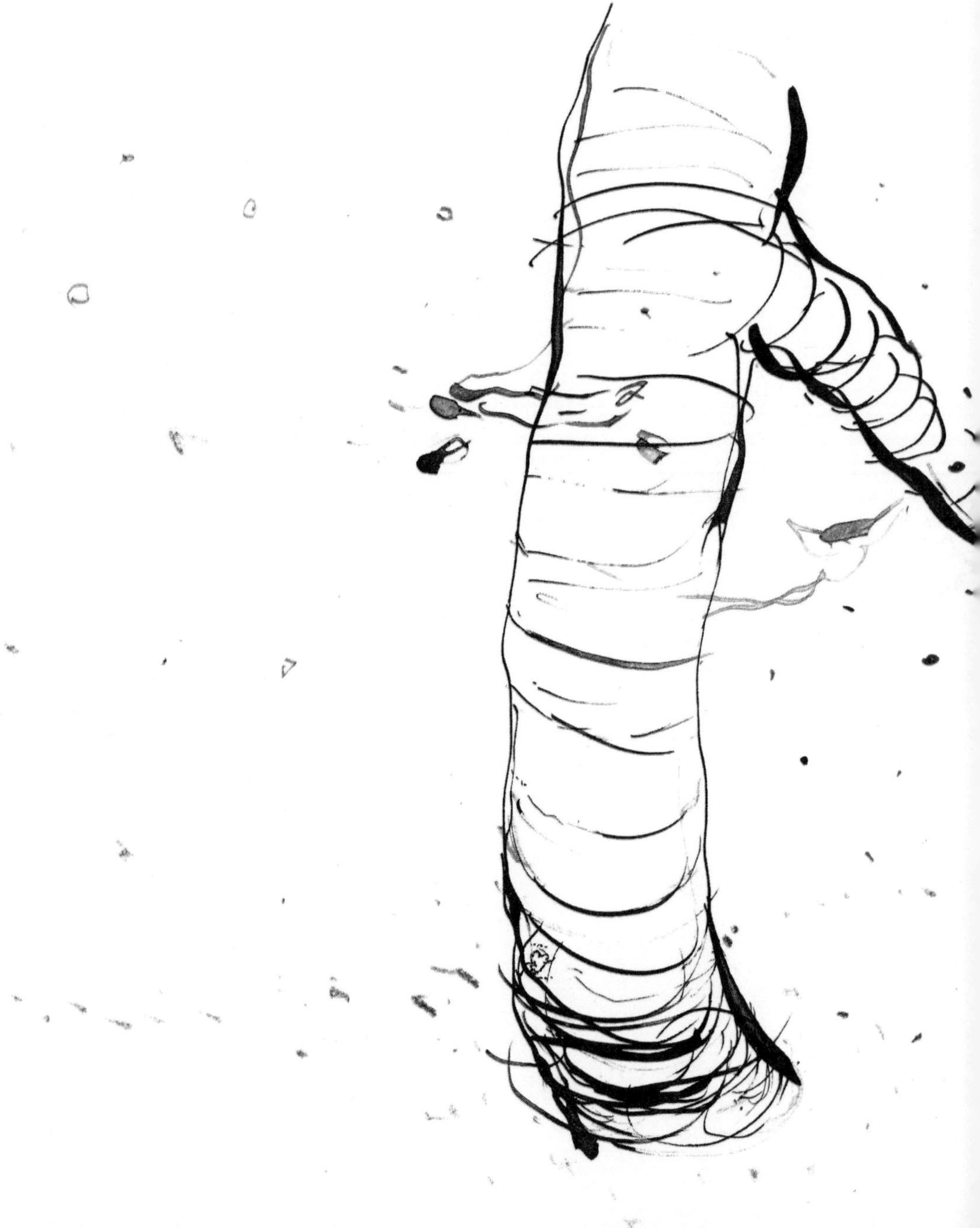

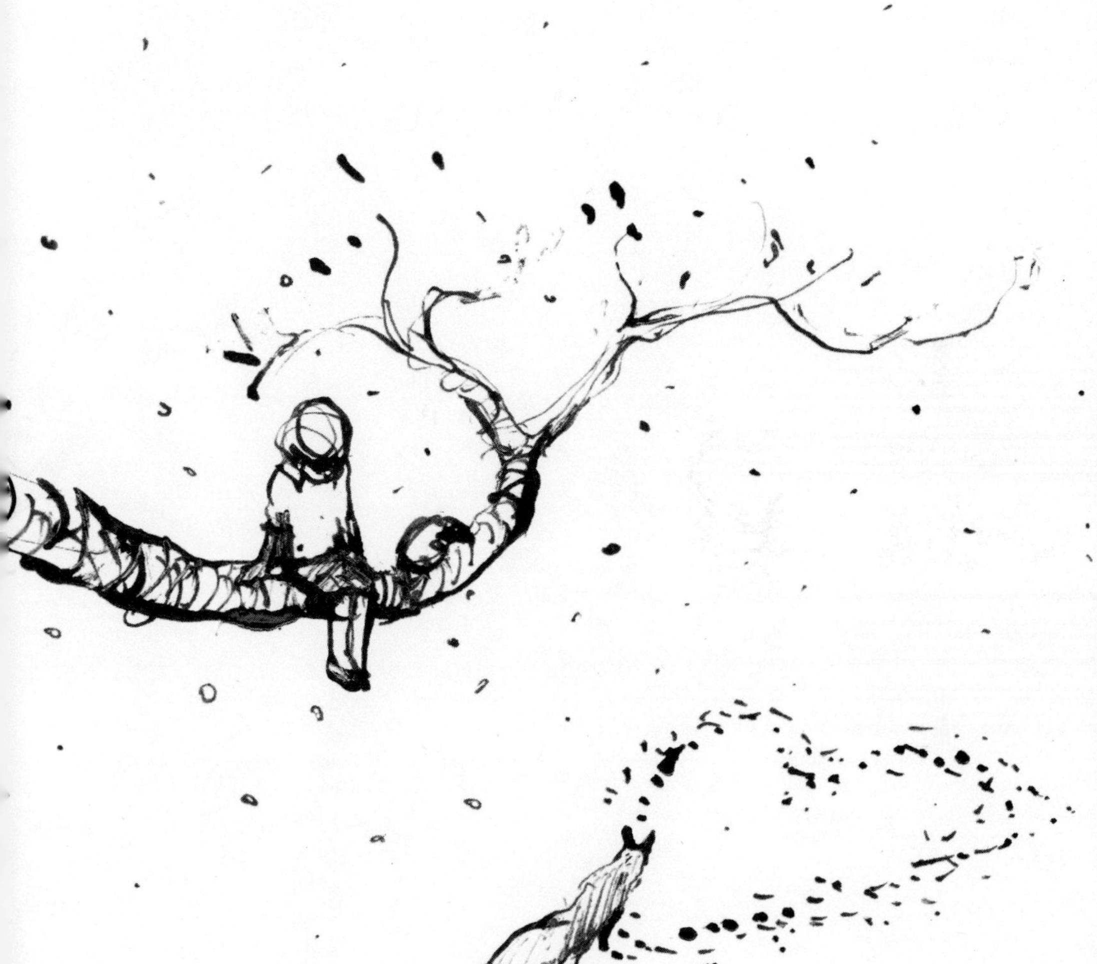

"I've learned how to be
in the present."
"How?" asked the boy
"I find a quiet spot and
shut my eyes and breathe."

"That's good, and then?"
"Then I focus."
"What do you focus on?"
"Cake," said the mole.

"Isn't it odd. We can
only see our outsides, but
nearly everything happens on
the inside."

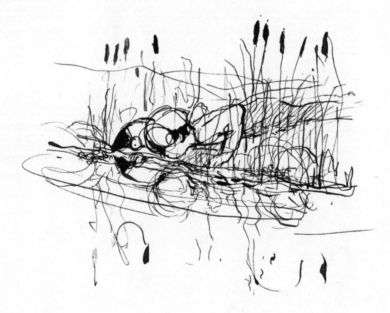

"Be careful not to fa..."

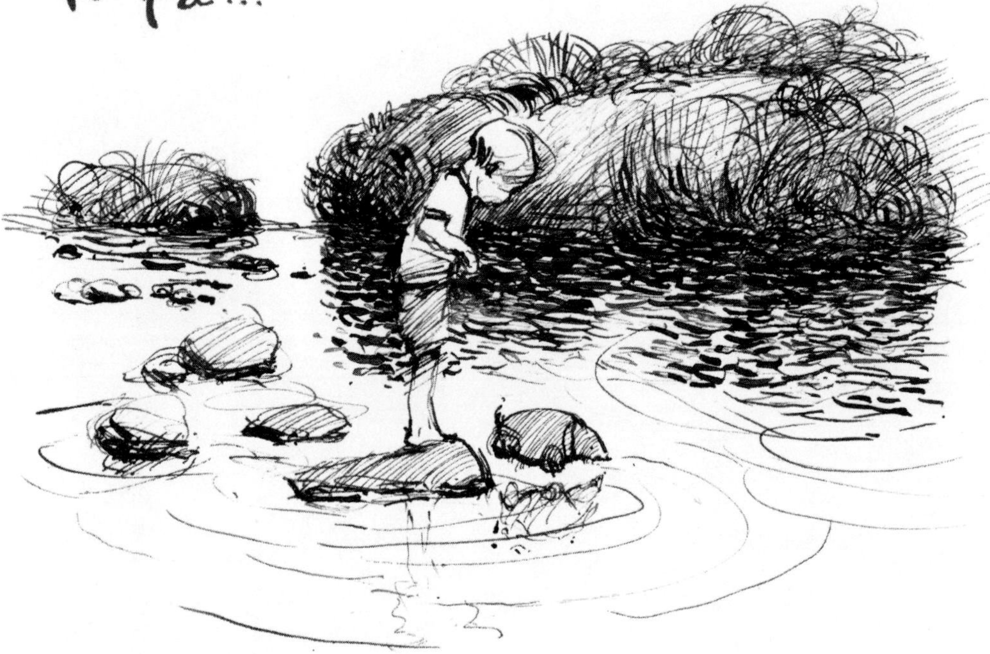

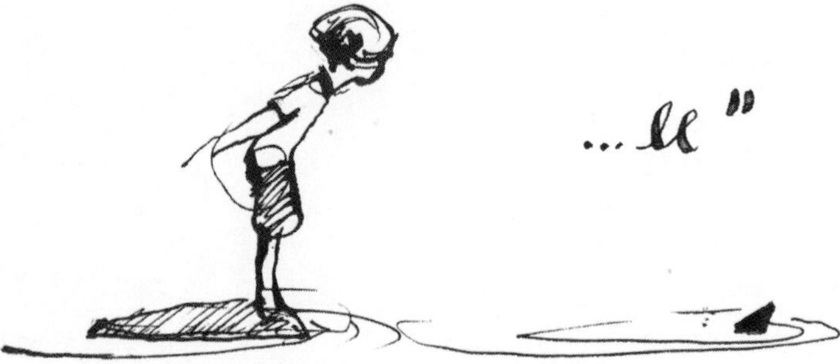

...ll"

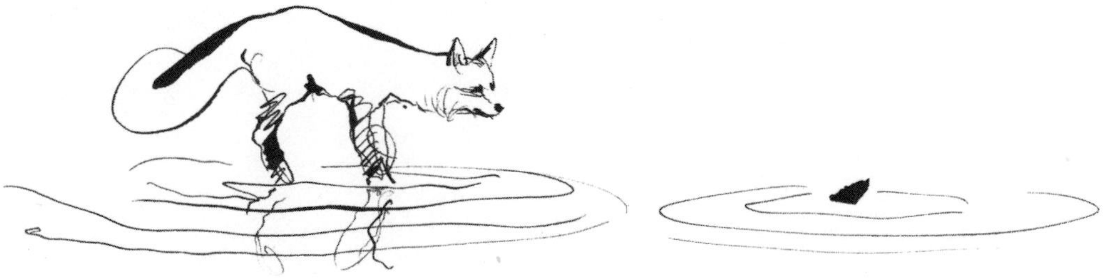

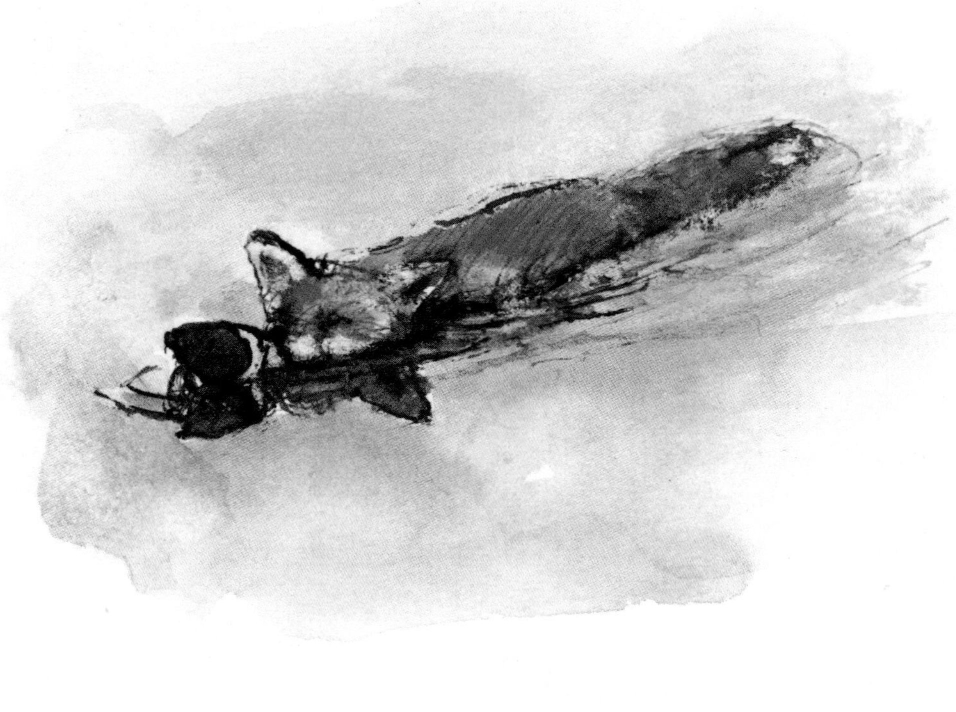

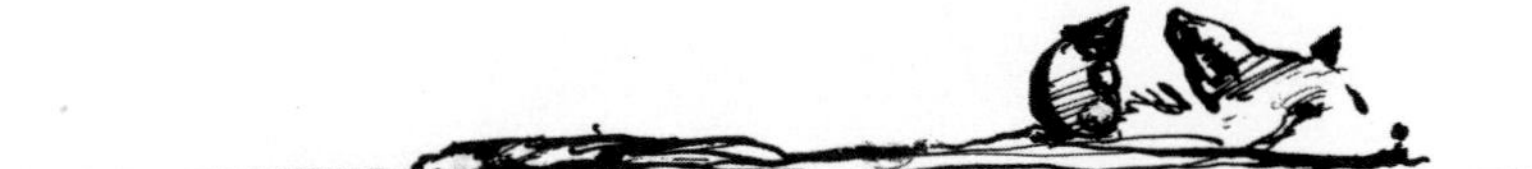

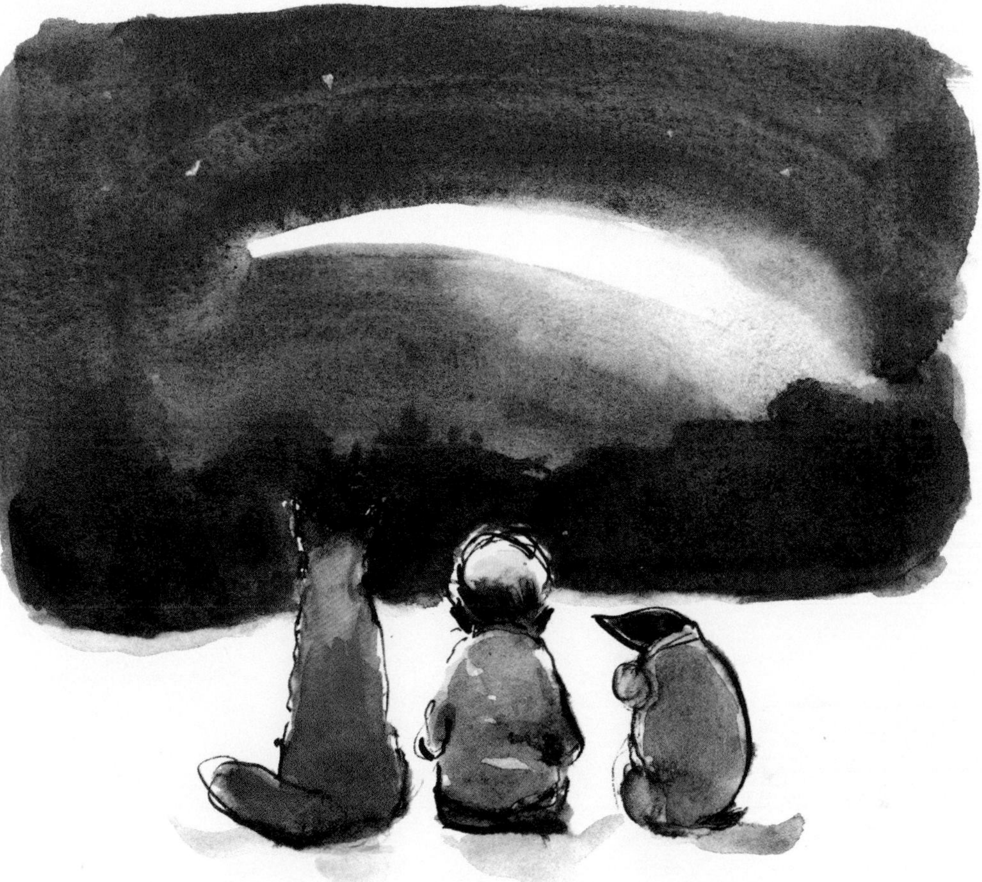

"So much beauty we need to look after."

"Being kind to yourself is one
of the greatest kindnesses," said
the mole.

"We often wait for kindness...
but being kind to yourself can
start now." said the Mole.

"Often the hardest person to forgive is yourself"

"Sometimes I feel lost,"
said the boy.

"Me too," said the mole,
"but we love you, and
love brings you home."

"I think everyone is just
trying to get home,"
said the Mole.

"hello"

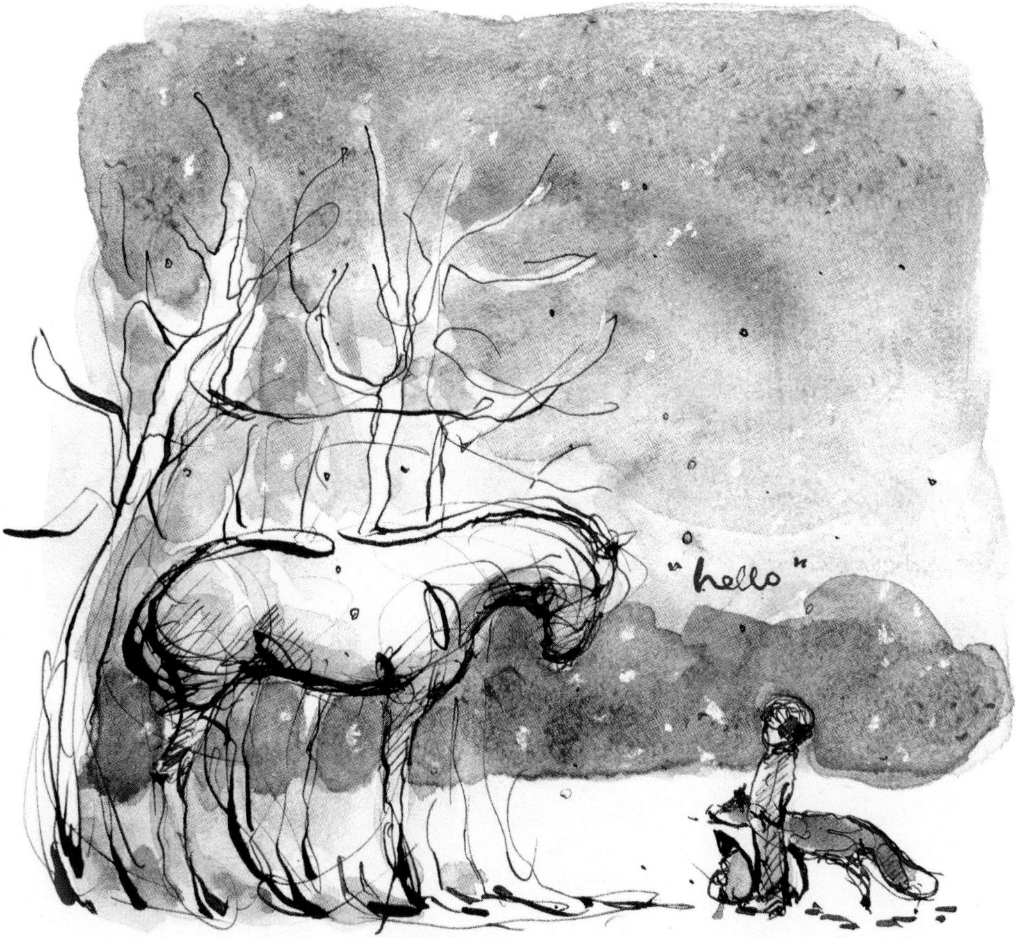
"hello"

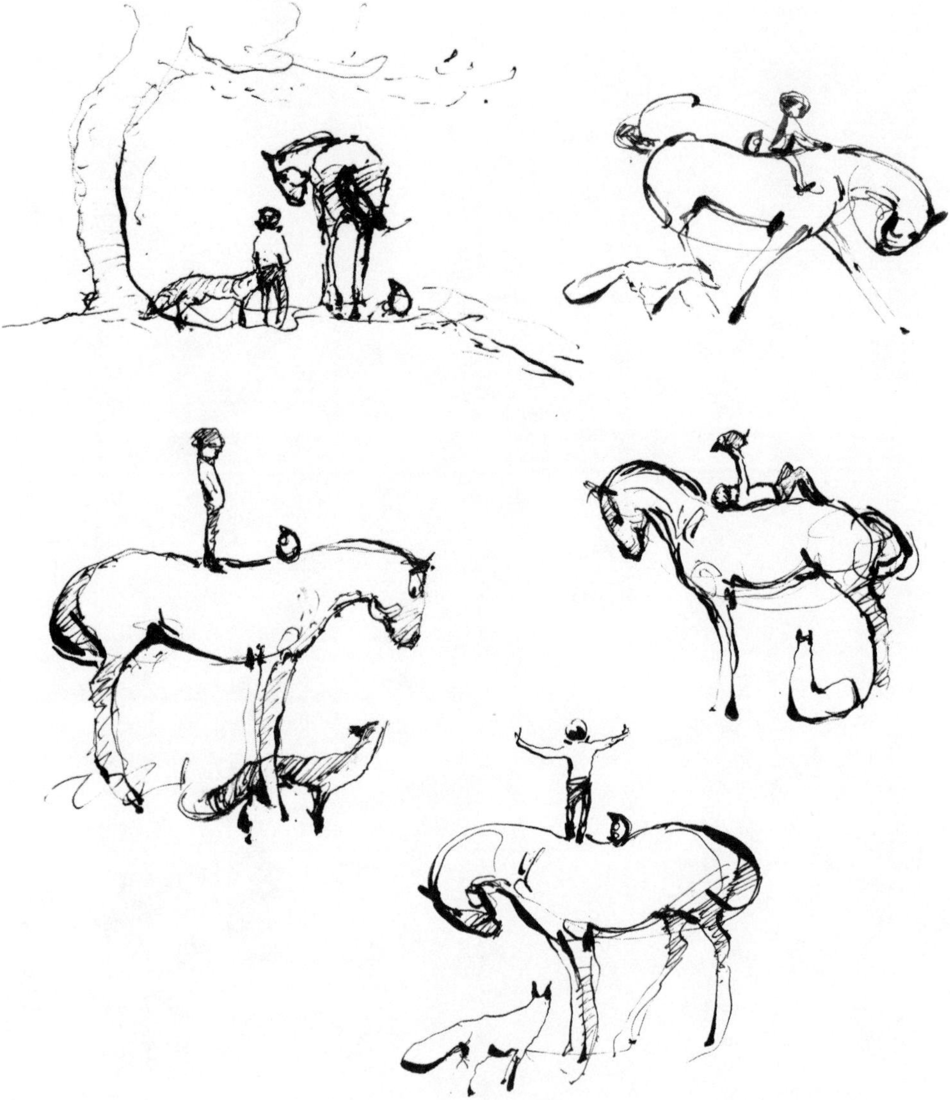

"Doing nothing with friends is never
doing nothing, is it?" asked the boy

"No," said the mole.

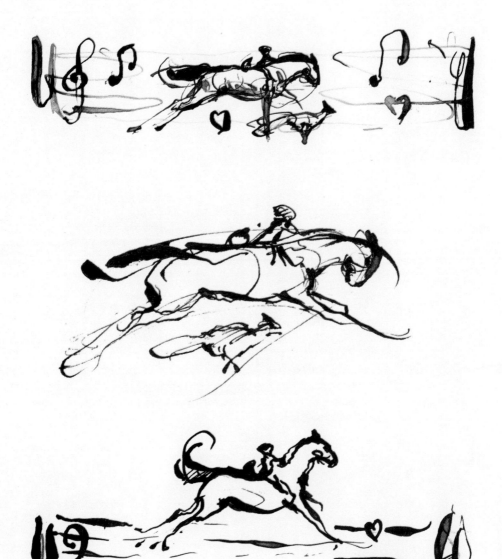

"You fell - but I've got you"

"Everyone is a bit scared," said the horse.

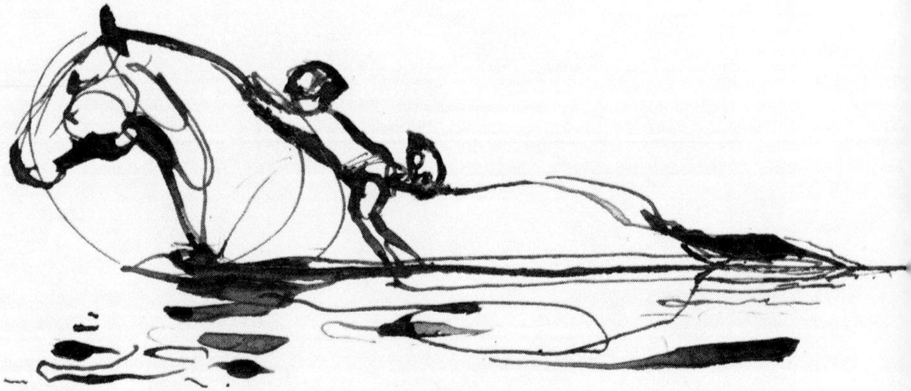

"But we are less scared together."

"Tears fall for a reason and they are your strength not weakness"

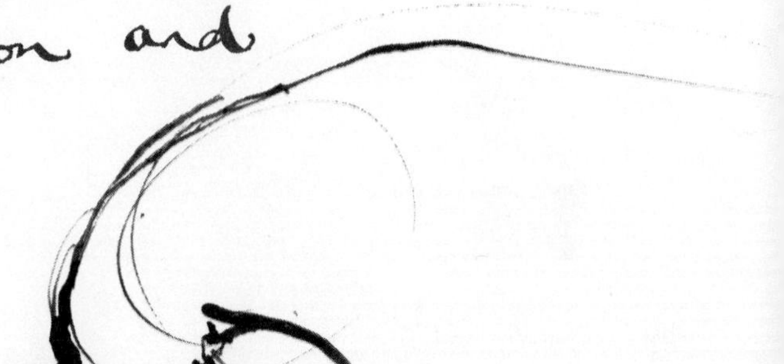

"What is the bravest thing
you've ever said?" asked
the boy.

"Help," said the horse.

"When have you been at your strongest?" asked the boy.

"When I have dared to show my weakness."

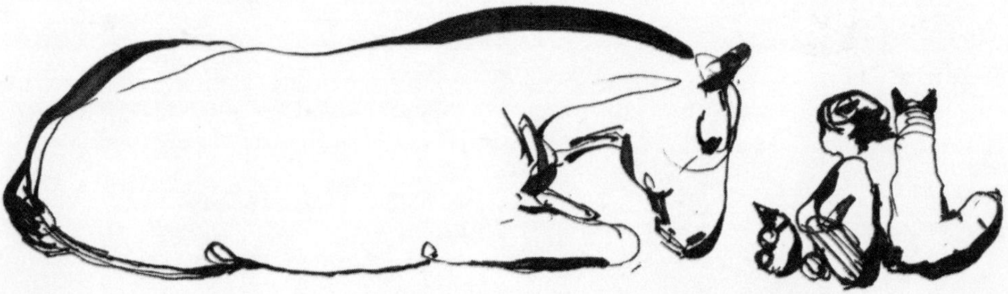

"Asking for help isn't giving up," said the horse.

"It's refusing to give up."

"Sometimes I worry you'll all realise I'm ordinary," said the boy.

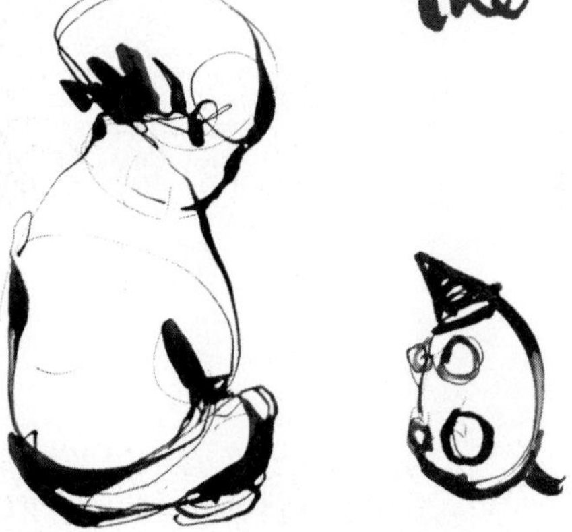

"Love doesn't need you to be extraordinary," said the mole.

"We all need a reason to keep going," said the horse. "What's yours?"

"You three," said the fox.

"Getting home," said the boy.

"Cake," said the mole.

"I've discovered something better than cake."

"No you haven't," said the boy.

"I have," replied the mole

"What is it?"

"A hug. It lasts longer."

"Nothing beats kindness," said the horse. "It sits quietly beyond all things."

"Sometimes," said the horse.
"Sometimes what?" asked the boy.
"Sometimes just getting up
and carrying on is
brave and magnificent."

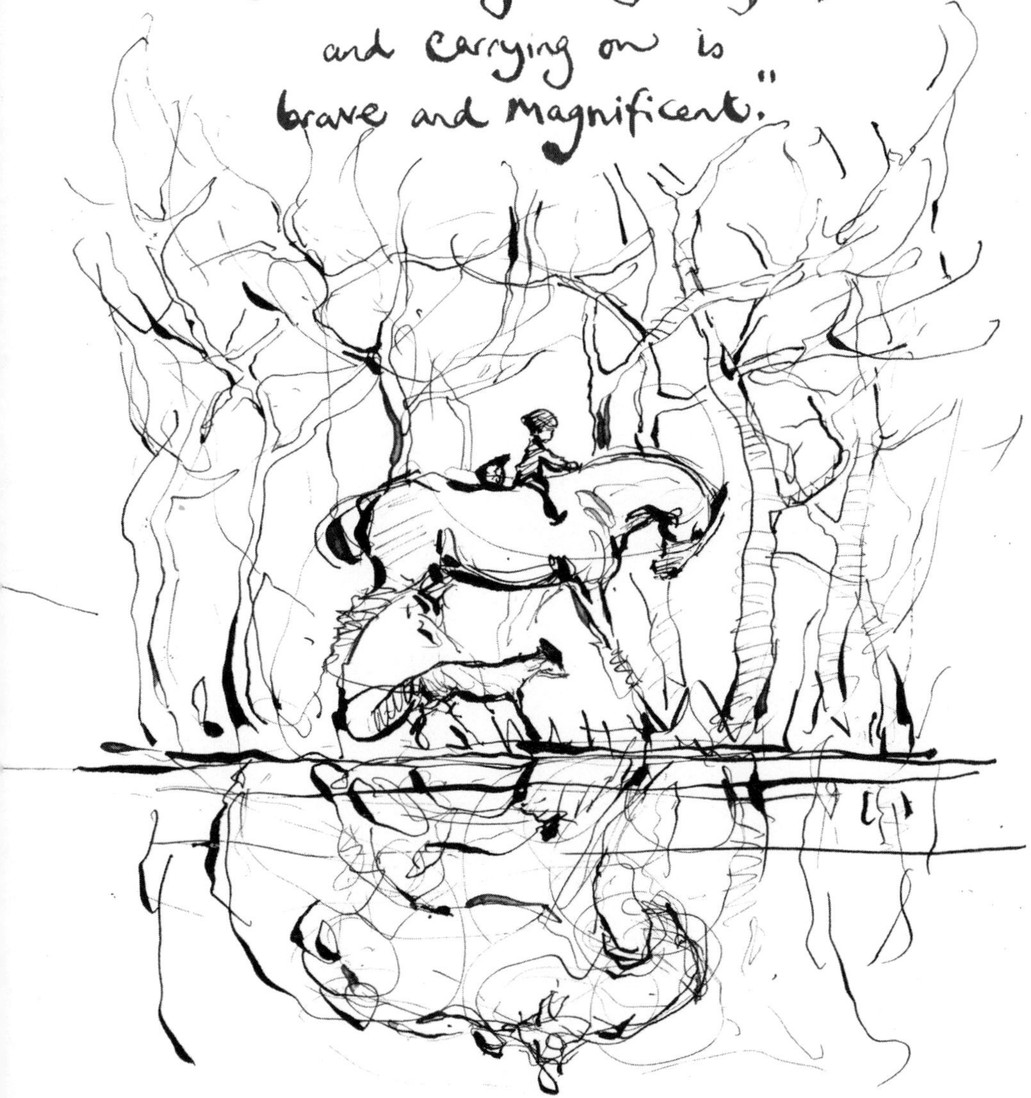

"How do they look so together and perfect?" asked the boy

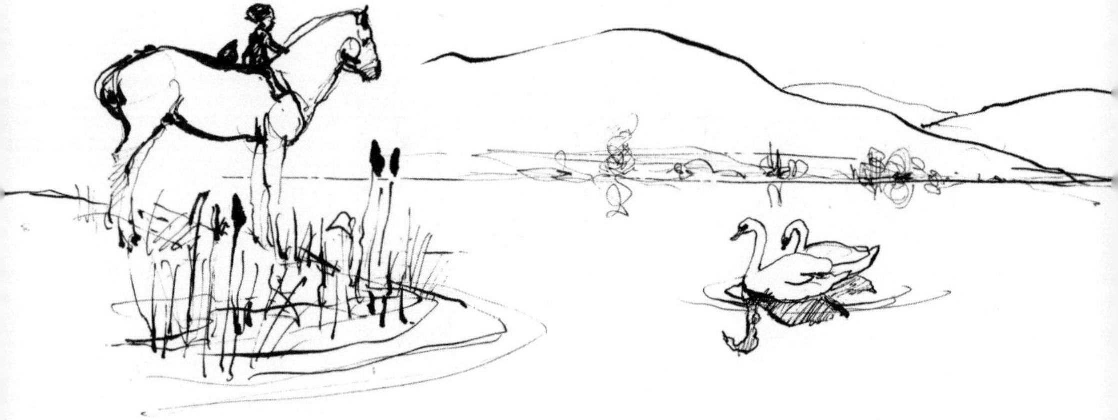

"There's a lot of frantic paddling going on beneath," said the horse

"The greatest illusion",
said the mole,

"is that life should be
perfect"

My dog walked over the drawing – clearly trying to make the point

"Is it the moon?" asked the boy.

"It's a tea cup stain..." said the mole, "and where there's tea there's cake".

Be curious

"Life is difficult -
but you are loved."

"So you know all about me?" asked the boy

"Yes," said the horse.

"And you still love me?"

"We love you <u>all</u> the more"

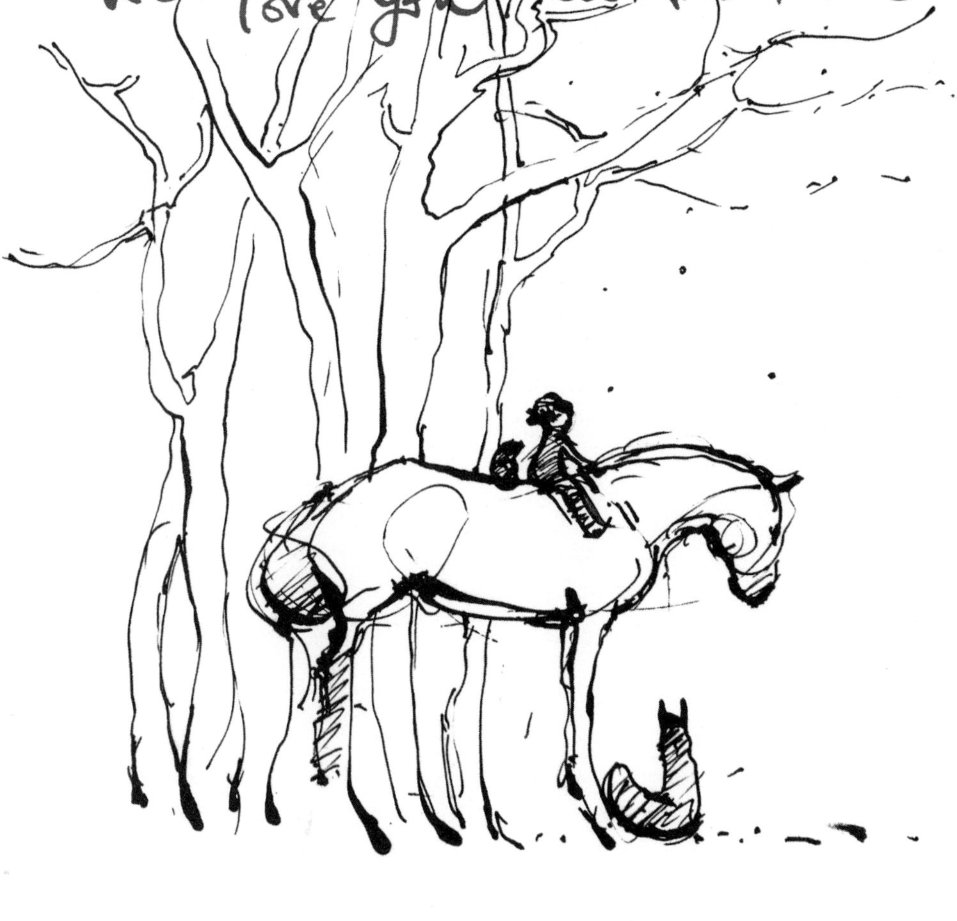

"Sometimes I think
you believe in me
more than I do,"
said the boy

"You'll catch up,"
said the horse

"The fox never really speaks,"
whispered the boy.

"No. And it's lovely he is with us."
said the horse.

"To be honest, I often feel I have nothing interesting to say," said the fox.

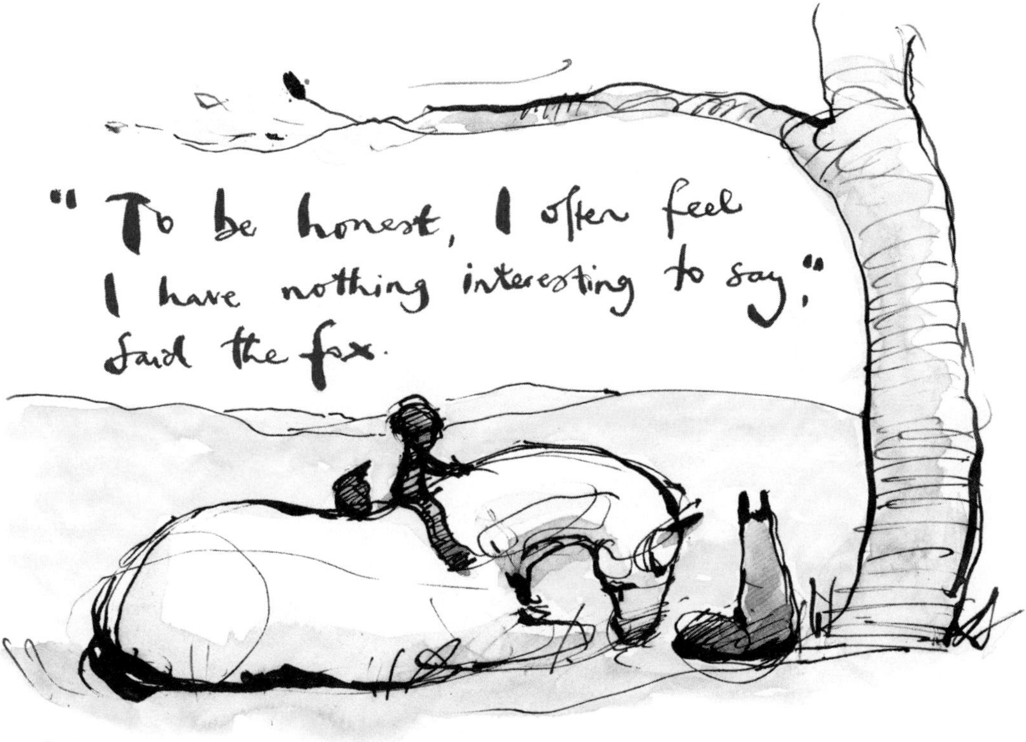

"Being honest is always interesting," said the horse.

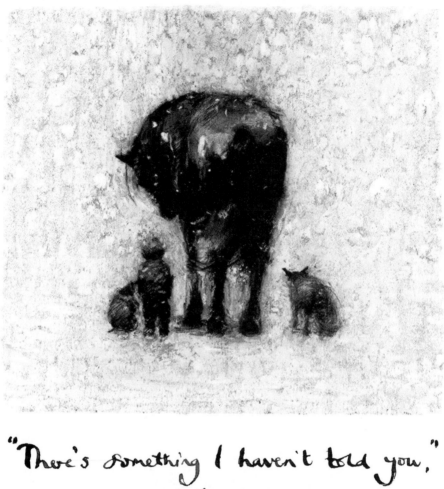

"There's something I haven't told you,"
said the horse,
"What's that?" said the boy
"I can fly. but I stopped because
it made other horses jealous."

"Well we love you

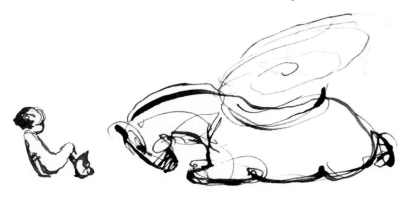

whether you can fly or not."

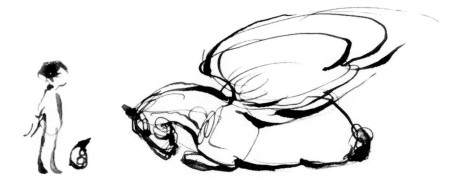

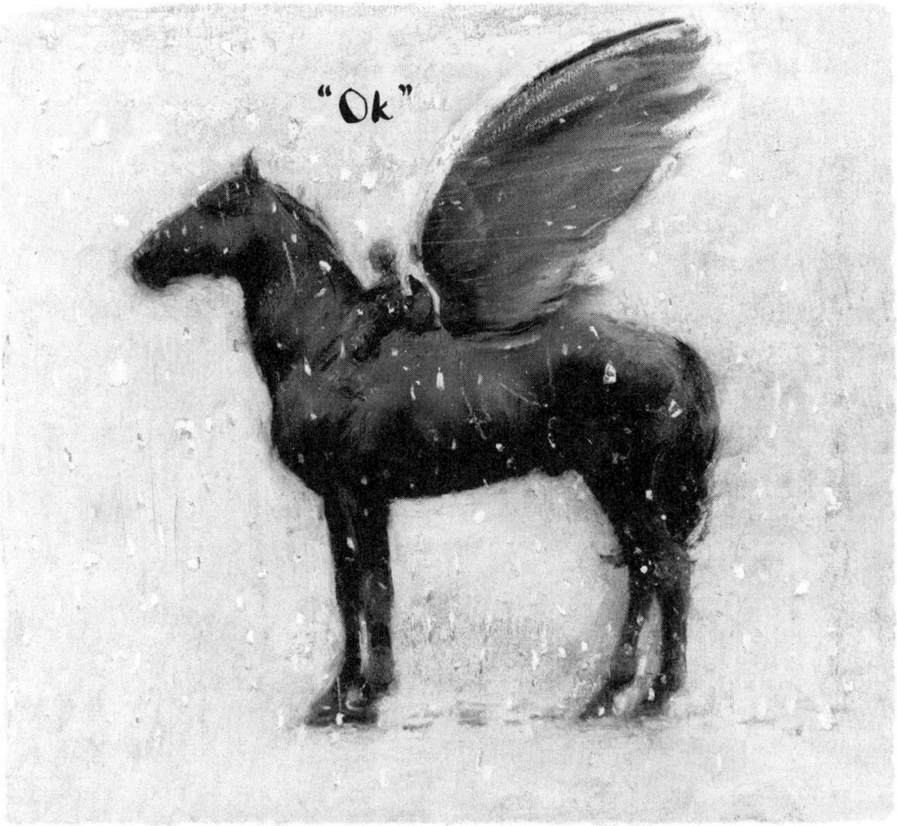
"Ok"

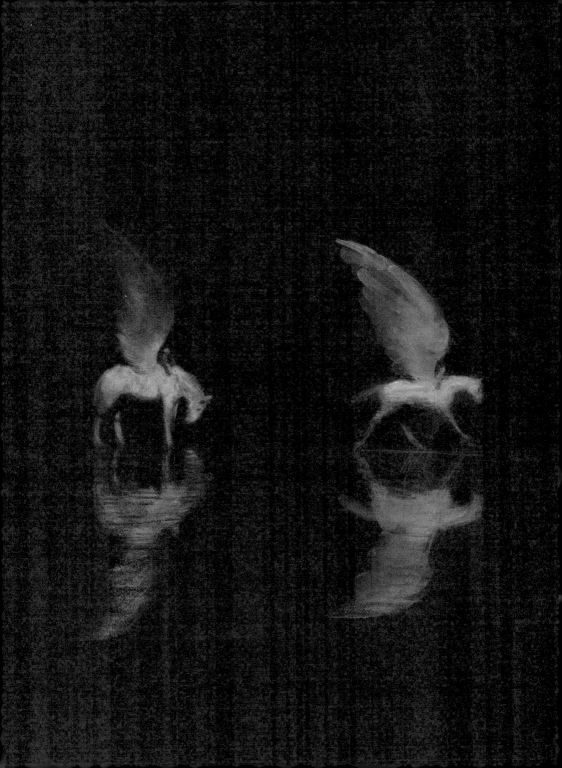

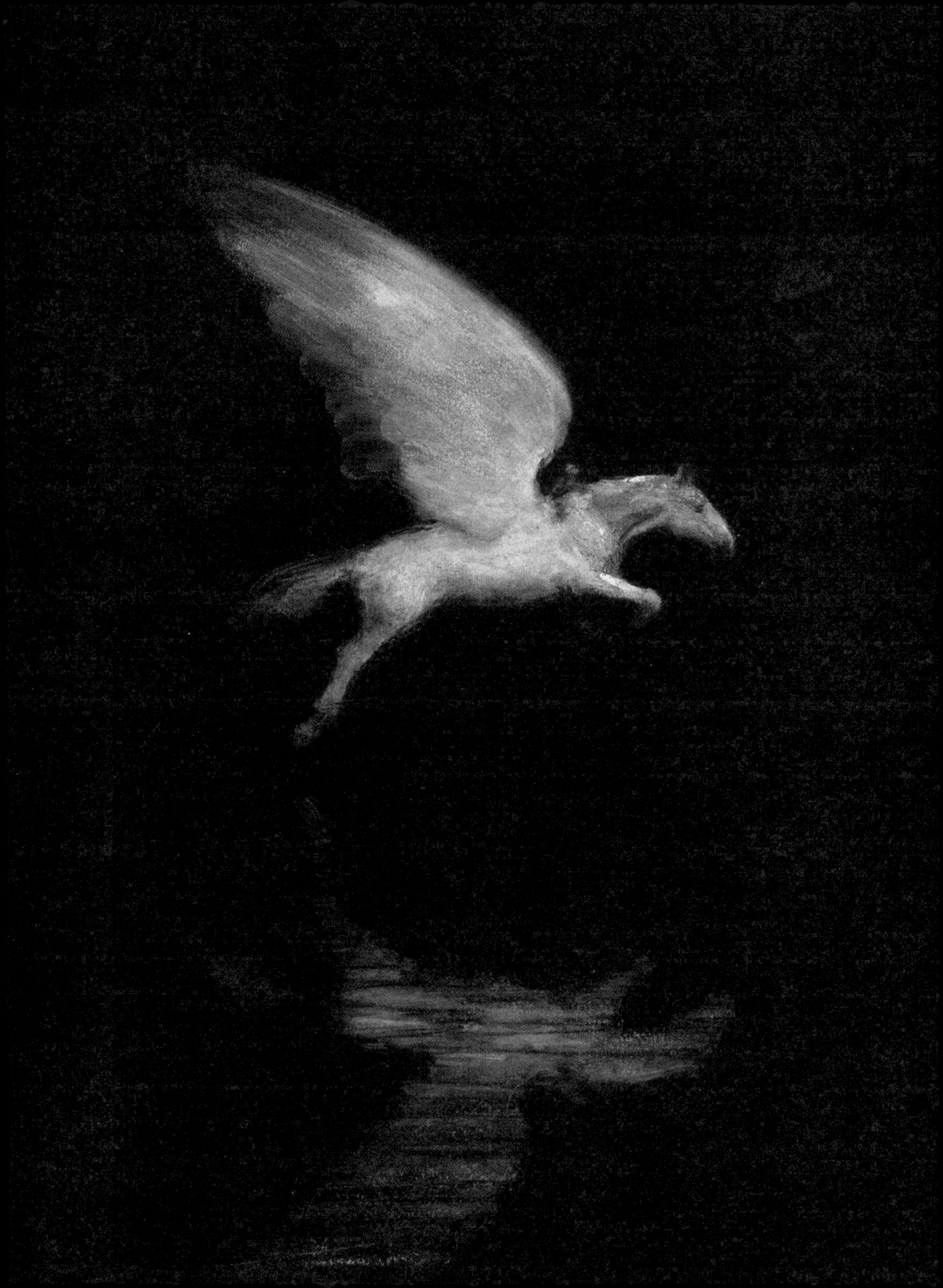

"Is your glass half empty or half full?"
asked the mole.
"I think I'm grateful to have a glass,"
said the boy

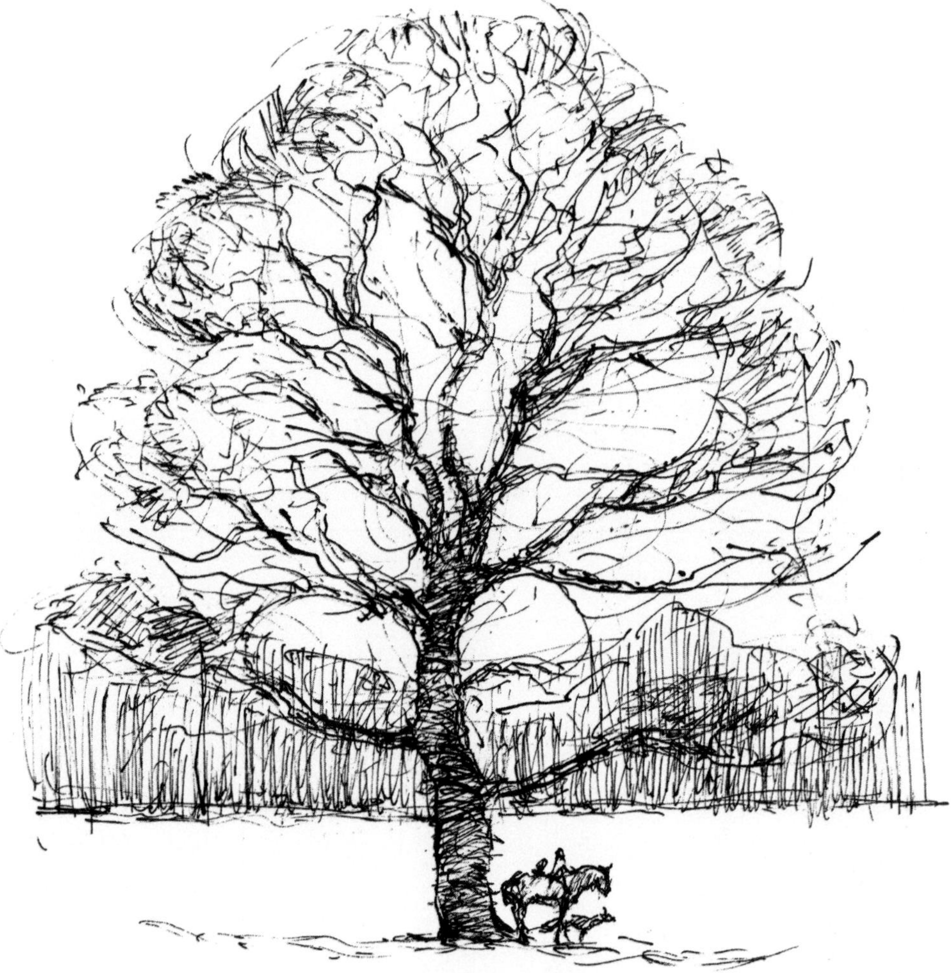

"We don't know about tomorrow," said the horse, "all we need to know is that we love each other."

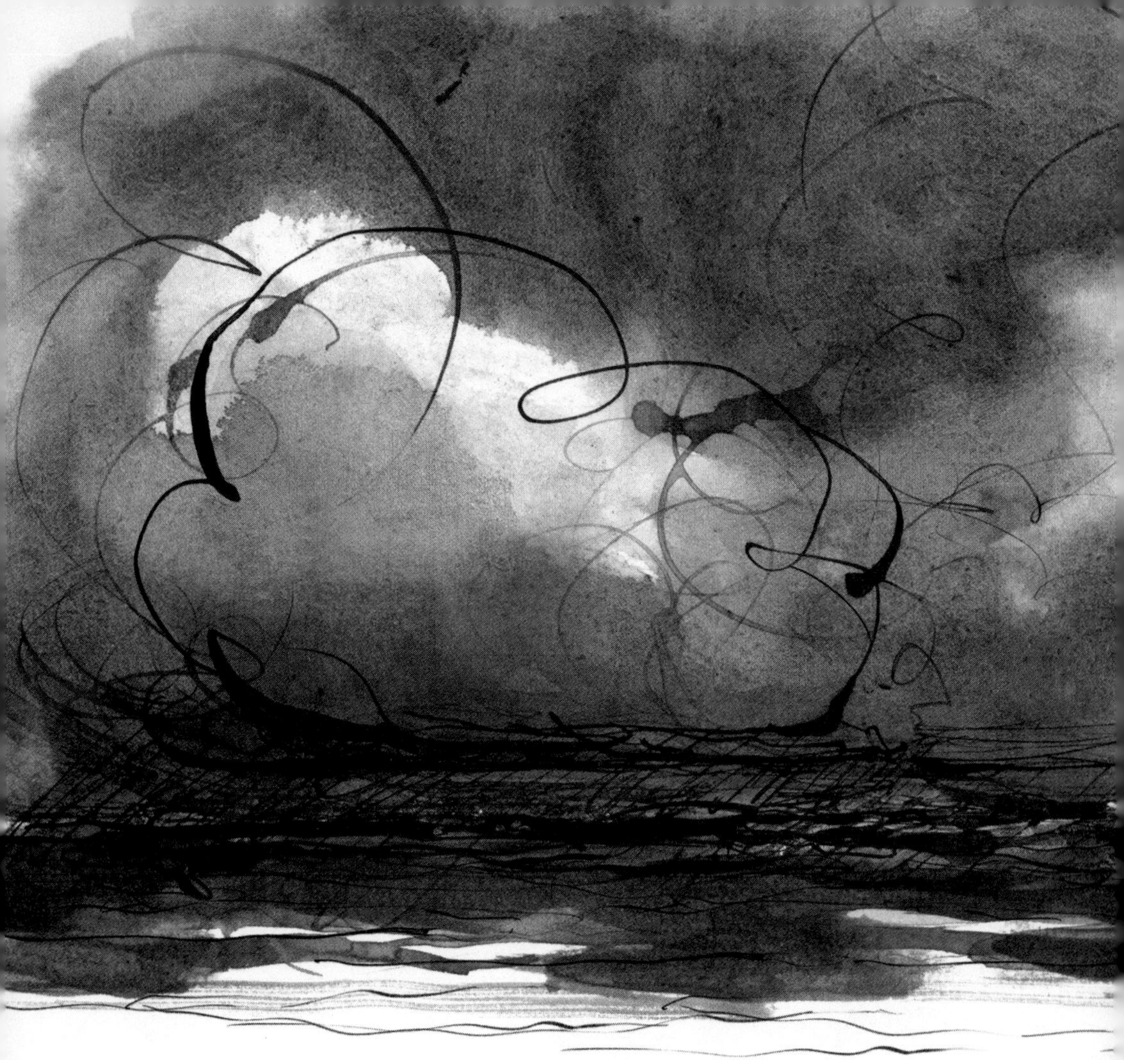

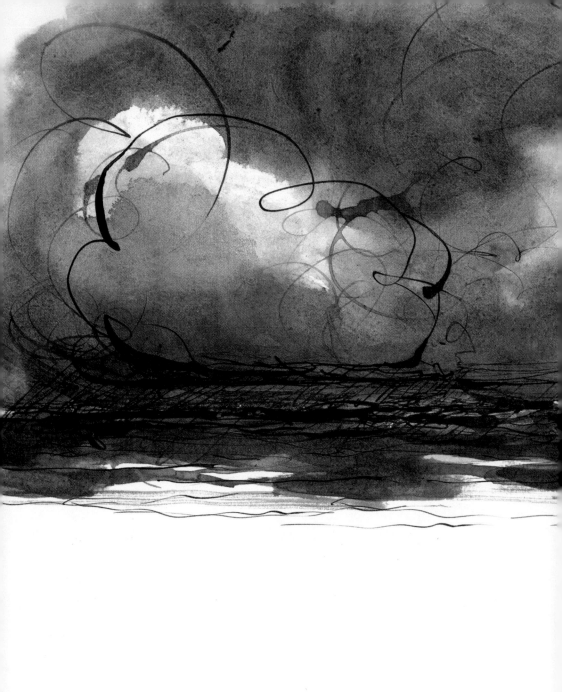

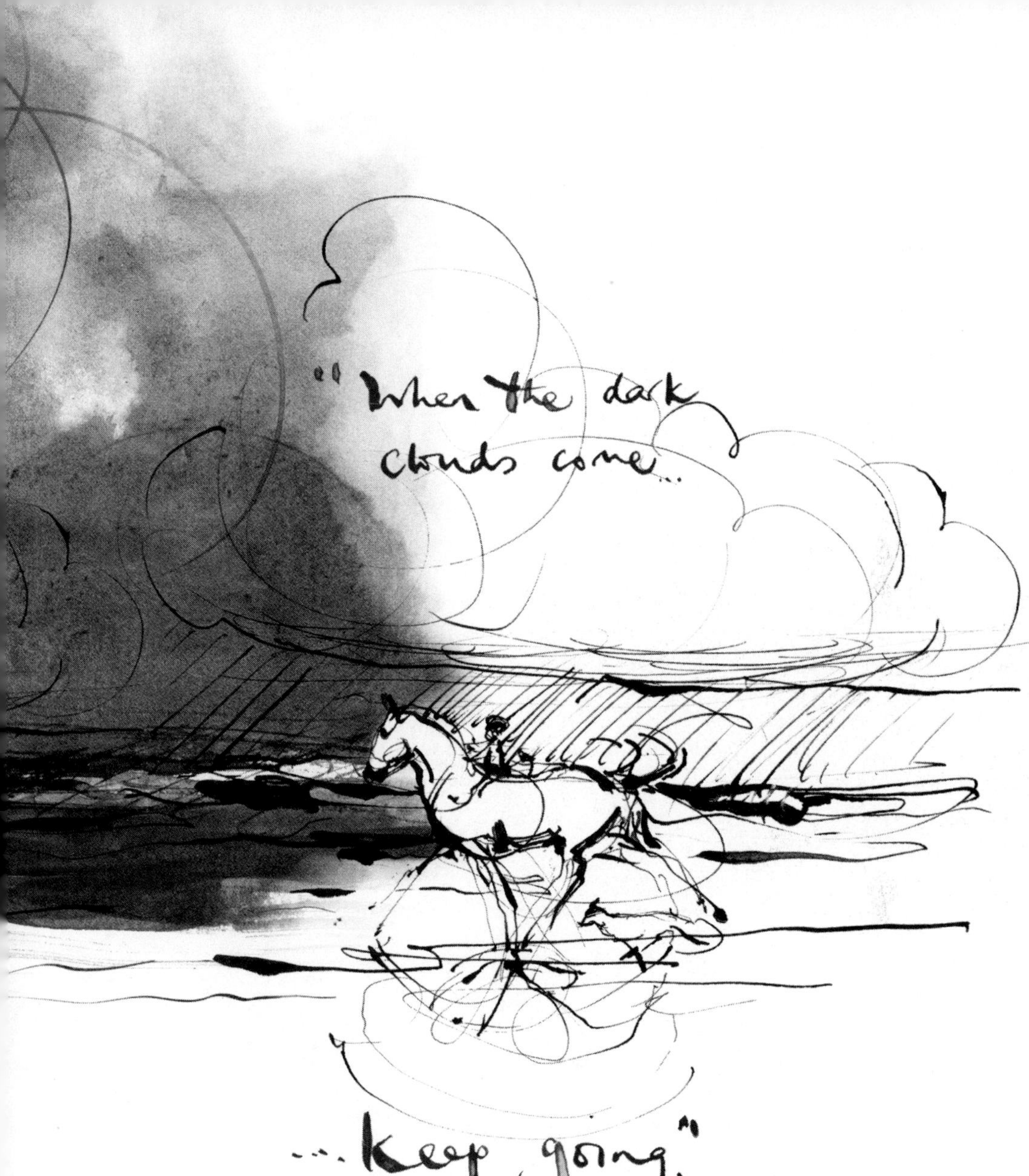
"When the dark clouds come...
...keep going."

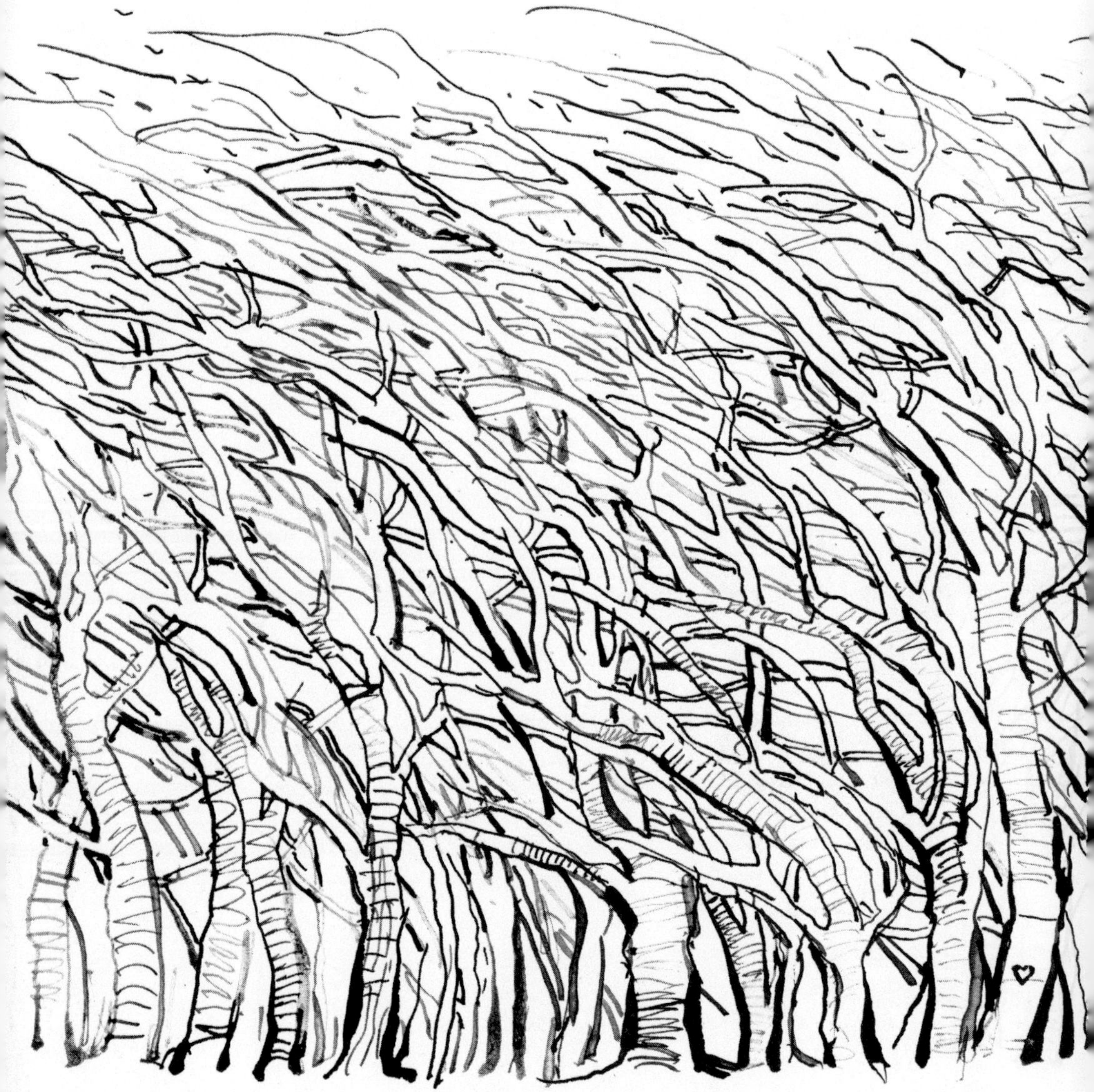

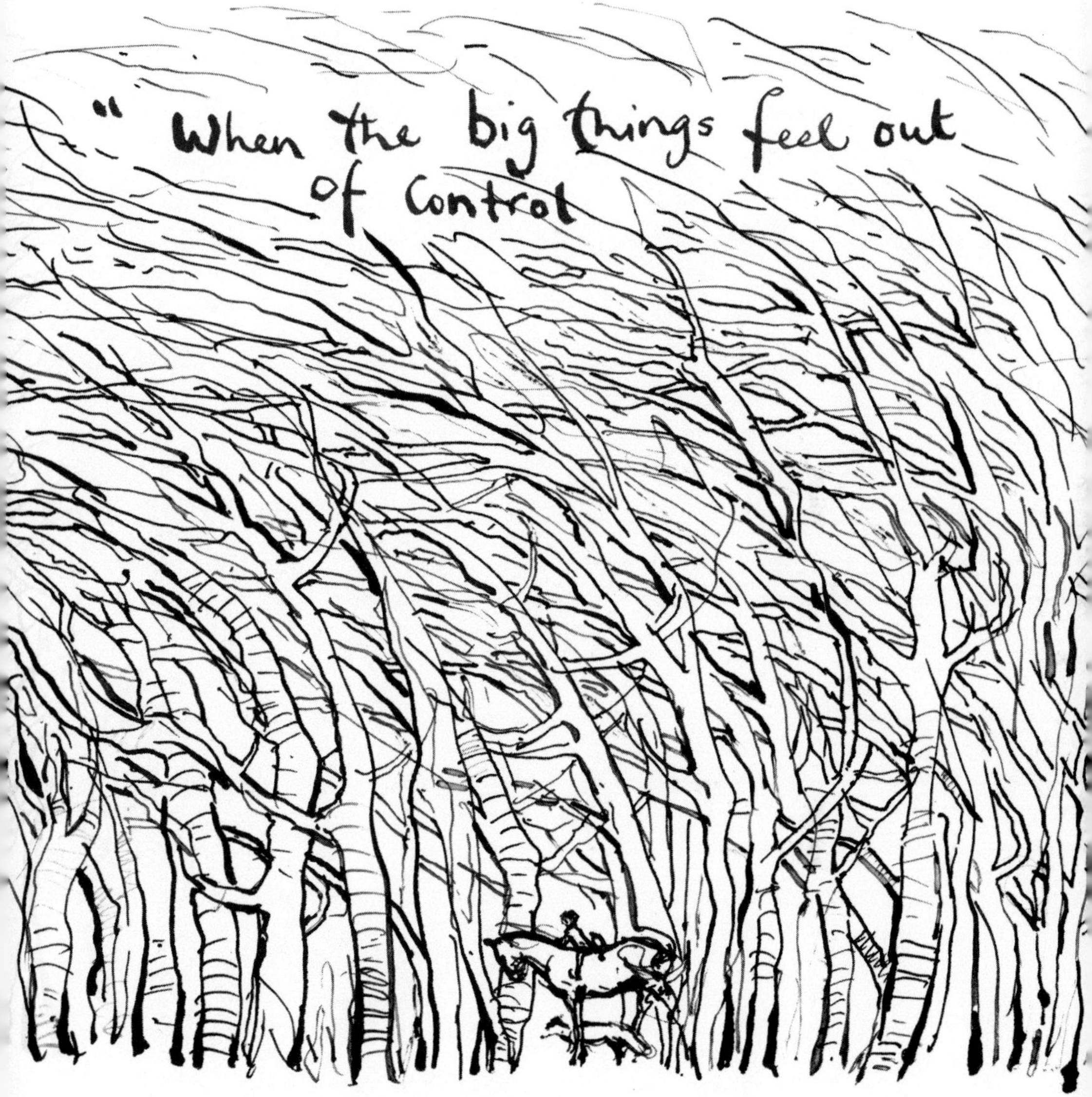
"When the big things feel out of control

... focus on what you love right under your nose."

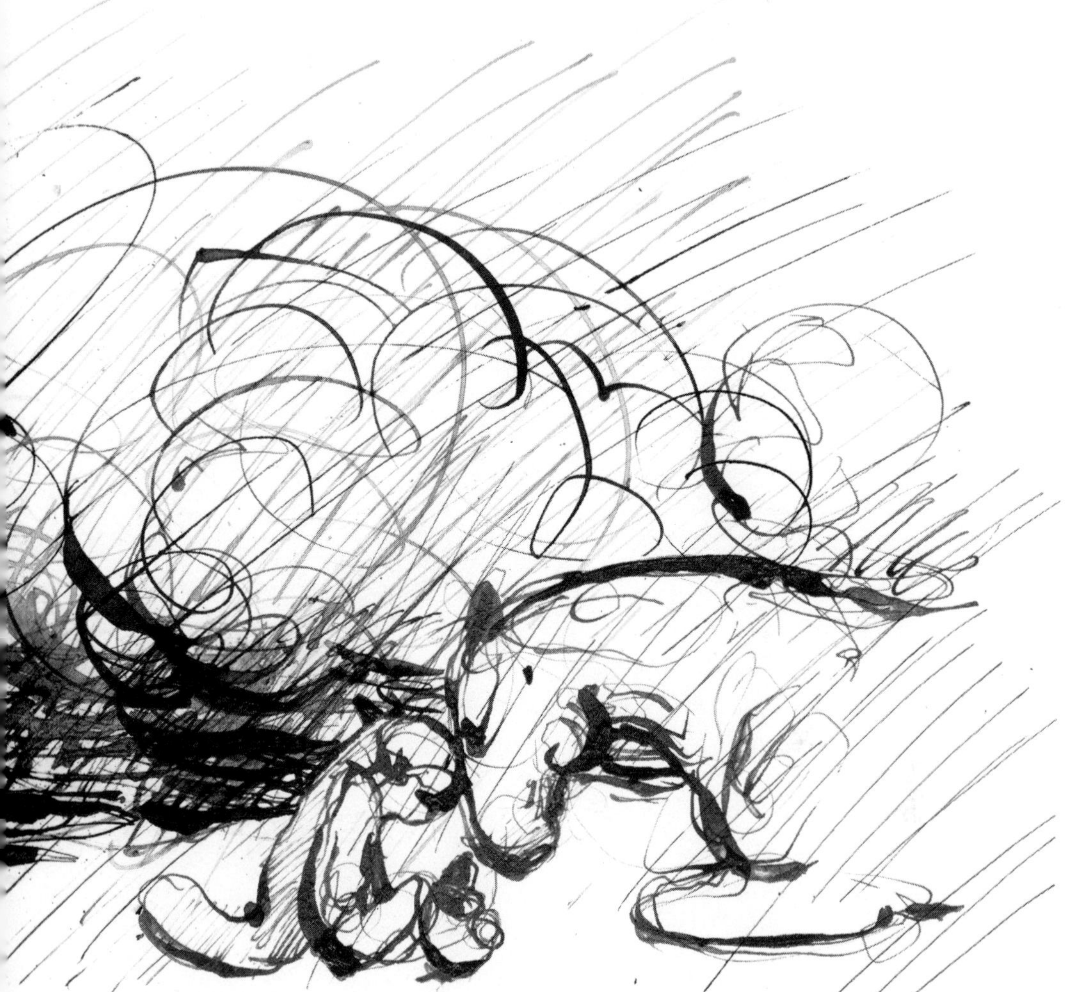

"This storm will pass."

After the Storm

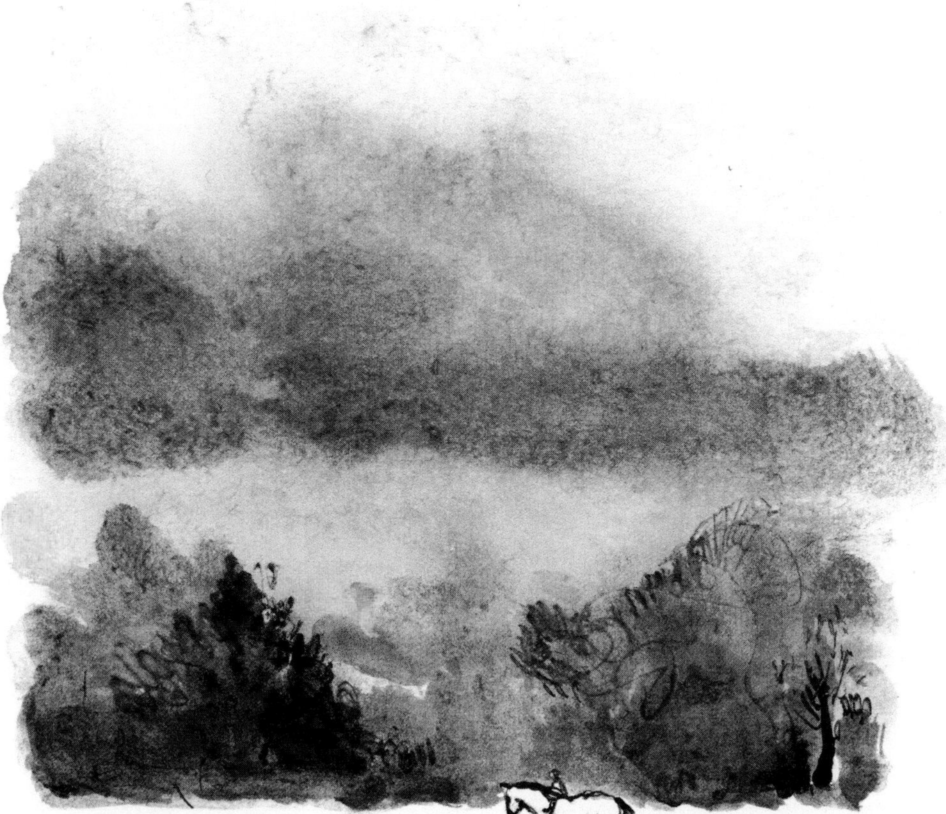

"We have such a long way to go," sighed the boy.

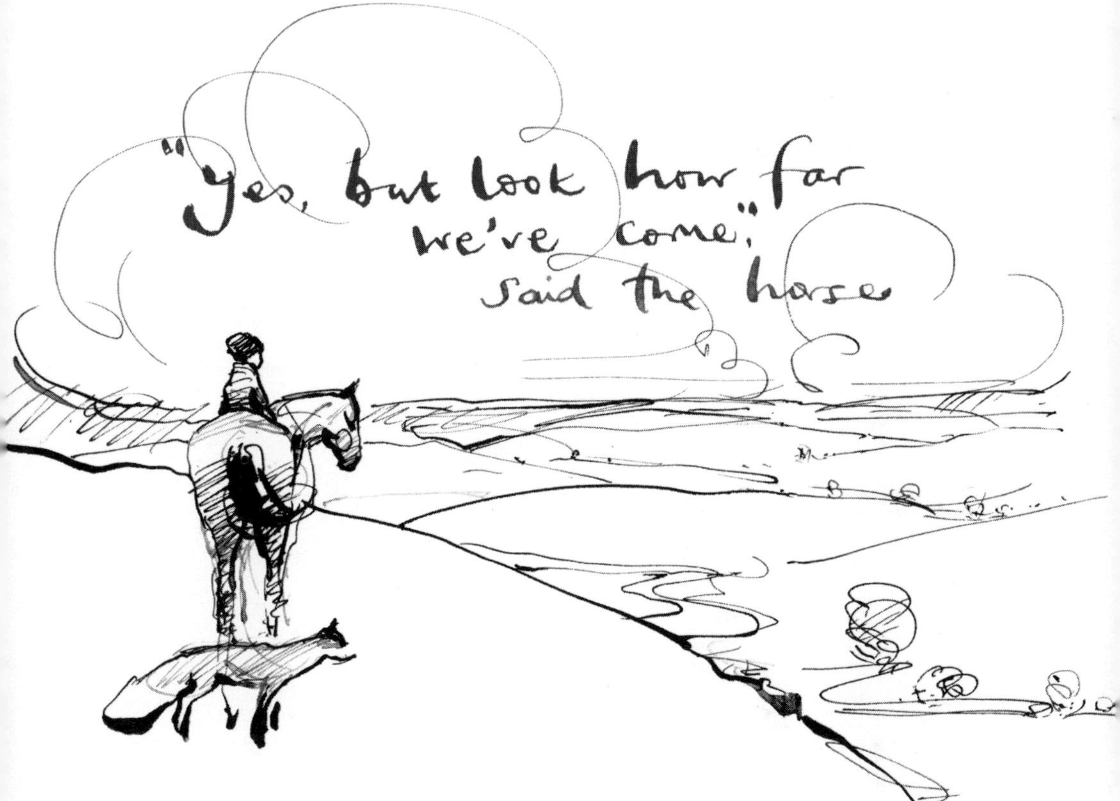
"Yes, but look how far we've come," said the horse

"Sometimes I want to say I love you all," said the mole, "but I find it difficult."

"Do you?" said the boy.

"Yes, so I say something like I'm glad we are all here."

"OK," said the boy.

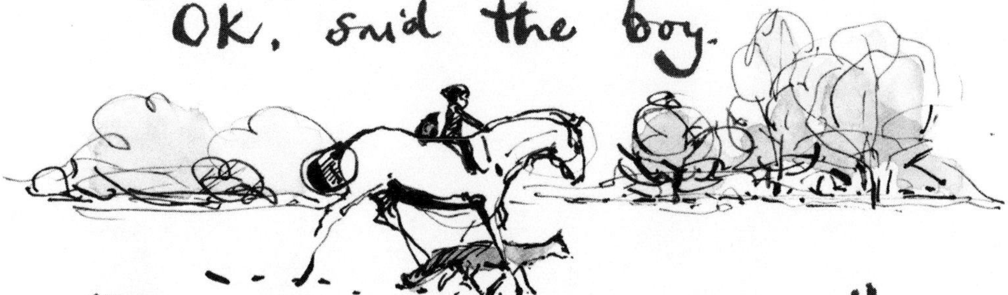

"I'm glad we are all here."

"We are so glad you are here too."

"What's your best discovery?" asked the mole.

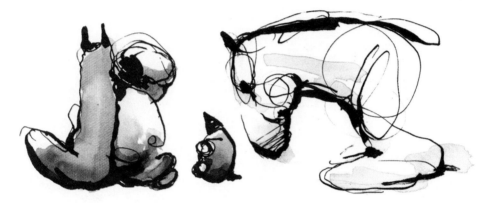

"That I'm enough as I am," said the boy.

"I've realised why we are here,"
whispered the boy.
"For cake?" asked the mole.

"To love," said the boy.
"And be loved," said the horse.

"What do we do when our hearts hurt?" asked the boy

"We wrap them with friendship, shared tears and time, till they wake hopeful and happy again."

"Do you have any other advice?"
asked the boy

"Don't measure how valuable you
are by the way you are treated,"
said the horse

"Always remember you matter,
You're important and you are loved,
and you bring to this world

things no one else can."

"Home isn't always
a place is it?"

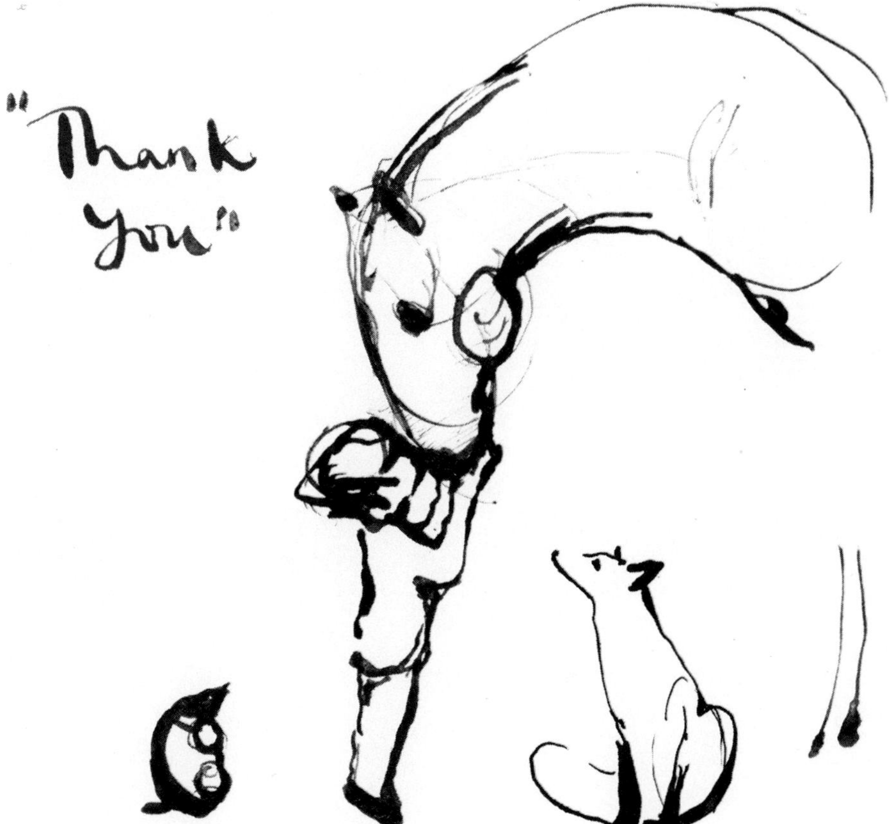
"Thank you!"

The ~~end~~

look how
far we've
come

"Sometimes all you hear about
is the hate,
but there is
more love in
this world than
you could
possibly
imagine."

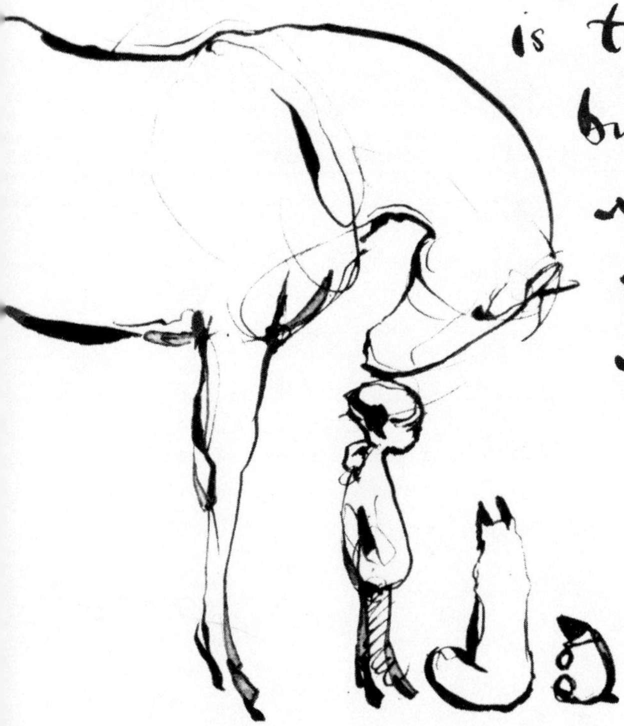

This book is about friendship and I couldn't have made it without my friends. So thank you Matthew, Grace, Bear, Phil, Miranda, Amy, Emma, Scarlett, Charlie, Richard and Helen to name a few, whose conversations and love are so part of these pages. x

Thanks to Colm the brilliant Irishman who helped sew this book together often late into the night.

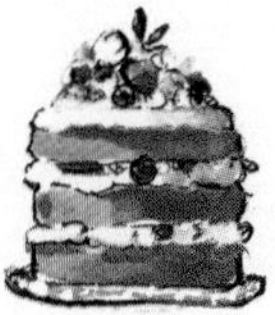

Thank you to everyone at Penguin; Gail, Joel, Tess, Becky, Lucy, Alice, Rae, Beth, Nat, and especially Laura who so kindly coped with me and my messy drawings.

And thank you so much to you on social media who encouraged me with everything.

Thankyou Sara, Daisy and Christopher for your love and endless cups of tea and to my dogs Dill and Barney x 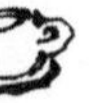

CHARLIE MACKESY WAS BORN DURING A SNOWY WINTER IN NORTHUMBERLAND. HE HAS BEEN A CARTOONIST FOR *THE SPECTATOR* AND A BOOK ILLUSTRATOR FOR OXFORD UNIVERSITY PRESS. HE HAS COLLABORATED WITH RICHARD CURTIS FOR COMIC RELIEF, AND NELSON MANDELA ON A LITHOGRAPH PROJECT, "THE UNITY SERIES." HE HAS LIVED AND PAINTED IN SOUTH AFRICA, SOUTHERN AFRICA AND NEW ORLEANS, AND CO-RUNS A SOCIAL ENTERPRISE, MAMA BUCI, IN ZAMBIA, WHICH HELPS FAMILIES OF LOW AND NO INCOME TO BECOME BEEKEEPERS. HE LIVES IN LONDON.

CHARLIEMACKESY.COM
INSTAGRAM: CHARLIEMACKESY

HarperOne

HarperCollins books may be purchased for educational, business, or sales promotional use. For information, please email the Special Markets Department at SPsales@harpercollins.com.

First published in 2019 by Ebury. Ebury is part of the Penguin Random House group of companies.

First HarperOne hardcover published in 2019.

FIRST EDITION

Library of Congress Cataloging-in-Publication Data has been applied for.

ISBN 978-0-06-297658-1

21 22 23 LSC 24

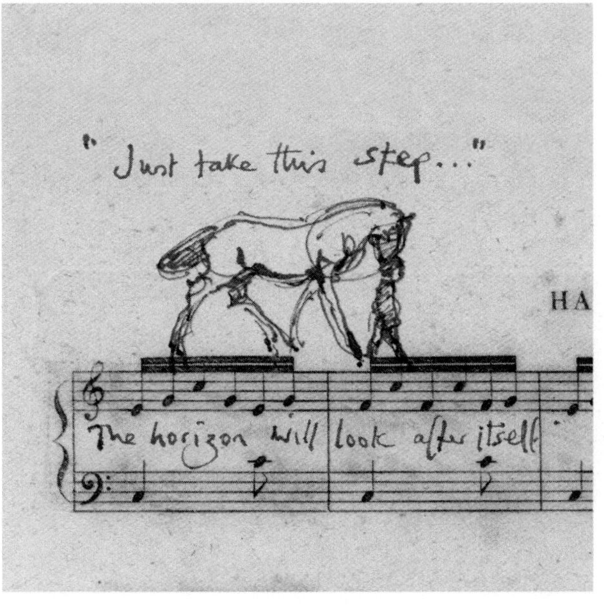
"Just take this step..."
HA
The horizon will look after itself